DIS

Japan's Technological Challenge to the West, 1950 -1974: Motivation and Accomplishment

The MIT Press
Cambridge, Massachusetts,
and London, England

Japan's Technological Challenge to the West, 1950 -1974: Motivation and Accomplishment

Terutomo Ozawa

This book was set in IBM Composer Univers
by CCI Compositors,
printed on Finch Publisher's Offset,
and bound in G.S.B. S/535/99
by Halliday Lithograph Corp.
in the United States of America

Library of Congress Cataloging in Publication Data

Ozawa, Terutomo.
  Japan's technological challenge to the West, 1950-1974.

  Includes bibliographical references.
  1. Technological innovations—Japan.
2. Japan—Economic policy. 3. Japan—Economic conditions—1945-   I. Title.
HC462.9.095   301.24'3'0952   74-3268
ISBN 0-262-15016-6

To William D. G. Scarlett and
to the memory of Patricia R. Scarlett

Contents

Preface

Only about a quarter century ago, the future of Japan was so uncertain
that no one could envisage the sudden economic growth that immediately
ensued. Now one can find a growing volume of literature, ranging from
journalistic to pedantic, probing the secrets of Japan's economic miracle.
Among the trailblazing publications was a special survey by The Economist
(Norman Macrae, "Consider Japan," September 1, 1962). Five years
later Macrae published another survey in the same magazine ("The Risen
Sun," May 27, 1967). In both articles the author not only admired, often
in a spirit of rapt fascination, the efficiency of the Japanese government's
economic planning and the vitality of Japan's private sector, but he also
suggested possible lessons the British economy might draw from it. In
fact, he stated in the introduction to his second survey: "It is with a sad
depression at opportunities missed, rather than with any proprietorial
pride of discovery, that your correspondent . . . comes back now feeling
like a Marco Polo with a strange and instructive story to retail of untold
mysteries that he has beheld in the east."

This book is devoted to a study of one source of these untold mysteries:
Japan's impressive advance in industrial technology. Japan's economic
miracle is attributed to numerous factors, but the momentum of technological progress, gathered in the course of assimilating Western industrial
arts and accelerated by Japan's own R & D effort, was a major force behind the waves of capital investment and continued high rates of economic
growth. Indeed, technological progress was the backbone of Japan's
extraordinary export performance in manufactured goods in the postwar
period, since it improved the quality and variety of exports and maintained competitive cost conditions. Without this technological advance,
Japan could not have fully exploited other favorable factors, such as the
undervalued yen and the freer trade position of the United States in the
postwar period. In this respect, Japan's economic miracle has actually been
a technological miracle.

The present study describes Japan's postwar experience in both assimilating Western technology and developing its own capacity to engender new
industrial techniques. It is concerned solely with the industrial sector,
although there has been equally impressive technological progress in the
agricultural sector. It should be noted, however, that the industrial sector's

progress and expansion made possible remarkable increases in Japan's agricultural productivity. As it happens, the agricultural sector played a relatively passive role in Japan's postwar economic growth. A study made by the Organization for Economic Cooperation and Development (OECD), for example, describes productivity increases in Japan's agriculture as follows:

The total agricultural production in real terms increased at an average annual rate of 3% between 1952 and 1967. Since the actively engaged agricultural workers declined by 2.5% on average per annum, this represents an increase in average labour productivity of 5.5% annually. In the same two decades the use of commercial fertilizers . . . increased by three times from 0.75 million metric tons on average in 1948–1953 to 2.14 million metric tons by 1967–68. This, along with widespread and intensive use of other sorts of current inputs (seeds, better feeds, insecticides, etc.) has obviously increased the land productivity and the output per hectare of the major commodities have risen impressively in the recent past.

The high rate of growth of average productivity of labour is due, to an increasingly large degree, to the increased efficiency of labour, as a rapidly declining stock of labour force is being equipped with improved tools, implements and power driven machines. The use of tractors and tractor driven machines has been put into use only after the fifties and their numbers are increasing rapidly. One interesting feature of the mechanization of agriculture is the adjustment of the scale and size of machines to the typical small size holding of an average Japanese farmer. . . .*

The expanding demand for labor in the nonagricultural sector induced rural workers, particularly the young males, to leave the farm for higher wages in the urban areas. The sharp decline in the supply of farm labor and rising wages led to the introduction of labor-substituting devices, including small tractors and other mechanized farm equipment, produced in the industrial sector. Thus the increase in farm output that resulted from the use of improved inputs and mechanization was essentially a by-product of industrialization.

*Montague Yudelman, Gavan Butler, and Ranadev Banerji, Technological Change in Agriculture and Employment in Developing Countries, Development Centre Studies, Employment Series: No. 4 (Paris: OECD, 1971), pp. 185–186.

Throughout the postwar period, Japan was fortunate to be in a position to enhance its industrial technology over a short span of time; that is, as a latecomer it was able to take advantage of the benefits of technological progress made in the West. Catching up with the West was the fundamental motive behind Japan's industrial drive, and a successful assimilation of Western technology was a key element in its success.

With this simple yet crucial hypothesis as the central theme, this book is organized in the following manner: Chapter 1 describes the postwar technological environment both inside and outside Japan. The Schumpeterian characteristics of economic development are identified, and Japan's double-pronged technological relationships—one with advanced Western countries, notably the United States, and the other with developing countries, especially in Asia—are examined. This unique set of relationships provided Japan with both a peculiar incentive and the necessary mechanisms to achieve technological advance. Indeed, the Japanese economy has functioned like a well-designed yacht skillfully navigated on the global ocean of economic development, carried by the favorable currents of Western countries' markets and technology, and pushed by the winds of the rising competition from developing countries. Japan's true source of vitality lies in its ability to adapt so dynamically to make the most of its unique position in the world economy.

The government-controlled program to import technology, which was initiated in 1950, and the trend of technology imports are examined in detail in Chapter 2. Favorable supply conditions existed for the importation of Western technology. The chapter considers those factors that induced Western manufacturers to supply technology even at the risk of fostering Japanese competition.

Chapter 3 focuses on the 1950s, the first decade of Japan's effort to assimilate Western technology. The effects of technology imports on Japan's export performance, capital formation, and import substitution are analyzed. Strong evidence is presented that Japan's postwar export competitiveness and industrial growth indeed originated in its assimilation of advanced Western technology and know-how. Chapter 4 presents a study of interactions between local interests, protected by the Japanese government, and Western suppliers of technology, who later became increasingly interested in setting up manufacturing operations in Japan. Japan's defensive measures against the advance of multinational foreign corporations are discussed.

Needless to say, Japan's borrowing and imitating of Western industrial arts was not done without effort. In fact, an enormous amount of effort was exerted to perfect the imported technologies, many of which were purchased in their rudimentary stages. Japan's capacity to make adaptive innovations depended upon its R & D effort. This and other features of Japan's R & D activity are examined in Chapter 5.

As indigenous technologies are developed and imported ones are improved, Japan is quickly becoming an important exporter of industrial technology, particularly to developing countries in Asia and now increasingly to Western countries. Japan's own technological advances are now helping it compete in the emerging multinationalism of the world market. The export of this new industrial resource and of direct investment capital from Japan is examined in Chapter 6. Chapter 7 analyzes the psychological factors behind Japan's economic drive in the postwar period and shows how the Japanese have reacted to the sudden changes in the world economic environment precipitated by the recent international monetary and energy crises. Japan's entire society, economic, social, and political, is at a crossroads; national values are now being reexamined and redirected. The new orientation of Japan's technological effort is described. The final chapter considers some implications of our analysis for the United States policy on technology. The effectiveness and desirability of controls on technology outflows to prolong U.S. trade advantage in high-technology products are evaluated. In short, the book describes the advance of industrial technology in Japan, shows how it has served as the backbone of Japan's postwar industrialization, and shows how it is coming to serve as a competitive factor in Japan's emerging multinationalism in the world market—all as a challenge to the West.

Throughout the book heavy reliance is placed on the official statistics and statements of the Japanese government—in some places even in an uncritical manner. Although they may be sometimes biased, important loci of

Japan's technological efforts can be outlined to facilitate our analysis and prognostication. The book is also admittedly of a journalistic rather than a scholarly nature since it often relies on newspapers and weekly periodicals. Yet the latest information about the subject matter can only be found in scattered pieces in these sources. An attempt is made to piece them together to construct a cohesive whole. The expositions presented here will possibly raise many more questions to perceptive readers than answers tentatively presented. I hope that any heuristic function that the book serves will exonerate any faulty analyses.

While the original manuscript of this book was being edited, the Middle East oil crisis struck and jolted Japan with serious repercussions not only on the future course of its economy but also, more importantly, on the political and economic relationship between the United States and Japan. I have added some observations relating this current development to my original analysis, but very cursorily to meet the publication schedule.

My interest in the present research dates back to the doctoral study program I completed at Columbia University in 1966 under the guidance of Professors Peter B. Kenen and Donald B. Keesing, to whom I am deeply indebted for intellectual enlightenment. Many parts of this book are based upon the findings of my previous research published in the following articles and monograph: "Imitation, Innovation, and Japanese Exports," in Peter B. Kenen and Roger Lawrence (eds.), The Open Economy: Essays on Trade and Finance (New York: Columbia University Press, 1968); "Should the United States Restrict Technology Trade with Japan," MSU-Business Topics (Vol. 20, No. 4, Autumn 1972), published by Division of Research, Graduate School of Business Administration, Michigan State University, reprinted by permission of the publisher; three articles in The Columbia Journal of World Business: "Japan Exports Technology to Asian LDCs" (Vol. VI, No. 1, Jan.-Feb., 1971), "Japan's Technology Now Challenges the West" (Vol. VII, No. 2, Mar.-Apr., 1972), and "Multinationalism: Japanese Style" (Vol. VII, No. 6, Nov.-Dec., 1972), published by Graduate School of Business Administration, Columbia University; and Transfer of Technology from Japan to Developing Countries, UNITAR Research Report No. 7 (New York: United Nations Institute for Training and Research, 1971). I also drew upon part of the results of my research report commissioned by the World Bank, Labor-Resource-Oriented Migration of Japanese Industries to Taiwan, South Korea and Singapore (Economic Staff Working Paper No. 134, International Bank for Reconstruction and Development, 1972). I am grateful to the respective publishers for permission to incorporate my previous works in the present form.

My appreciation is also extended to the Department of Economics, Colorado State University, which provided Xeroxing service. Last but not least, I am thankful to my wife, Hiroko, and our five-year old son, Tomoya, who, in the most understanding and cooperative way, shared the burden of authorship at home.

T. O.
Christmas 1973
Fort Collins, Colorado

1 Postwar Technological Environment

Schumpeterian Attributes

Since the end of World War II the economic life of Japan has undergone some astonishing changes. The gross national product, which stood at $10.9 billion in 1950, multiplied nearly 19 times over the next two decades and approached $200 billion in 1970. During the 1960s it grew at an average annual rate of 11.5 percent in real terms. This phenomenal growth has given Japan the world's third largest economy, next to the United States and the Soviet Union. Less publicized yet more fundamental than these quantitative achievements, however, are both the increasing sophistication of Japan's industrial structure and the improving quality of its output brought about by technological progress.

Japan's postwar economic growth has been so unexpectedly rapid and revolutionary in character that it is marvelled at as an economic miracle in the world community. War-devastated and ill-nourished only a little over a quarter century ago, Japan has metamorphosed into a modern country, hale and strong, with an economy that dominates competitive trade in world markets. An impressive array of new products was introduced one after another into the producer and consumer goods markets of postwar Japan: synthetic fibers, plastics, petrochemicals, special steels, electric and electronic products, copying machines, computers, and countless other new products. Roughly 40 percent of Japanese industrial output in 1970 was accounted for by new products, those that were included in the official production index only after 1950.[1] This greater variety of products was accompanied by new organizational and managerial techniques, new forms of communication and transportation, and new consumer services. Thus the newness of Japan's postwar economic life is truly far reaching. Joseph A. Schumpeter's description of economic development describes Japan's experience: "[Capitalist economy] is incessantly being revolutionalized from within by new enterprise, i.e., by the intrusion of new methods of production or new commercial opportunities into the industrial structure as it exists at any moment."[2]

Indeed, technological change has been far more extensive than the comparatively simple change in the quality of industrial artifacts. It is a socio-technological phenomenon in which Japanese society is totally immersed.[3]

Japan's capacity to adopt technological changes stems from its culture, the psychology of its people, and the historical momentum of its society.

According to Schumpeter, the recurrent development of major technological changes initiated by innovators and later followed by others "in swarmlike appearance" is the essential mechanism of an economic boom with a prolonged period of readjustment and adaptations.[4] Innovation is thus the prime mover for a long-run trend of economic growth since a vast amount of new investment ensues in the wake of each boom. With internationalization of business operations, innovations are disseminated at an accelerated rate not only within a country but also across national borders.

Japan's economic growth since 1950, following its initial reconstruction period in the late 1940s, was founded upon high rates of capital formation that resulted, in the main, from the continuous assimilation of new technologies purchased from the West. In the terms of the Schumpeterian paradigm, Japanese industry was engulfed en masse in a swarm of Japanese entrepreneurs who avidly acquired Western industrial arts. Since the technological gap was substantial, their effort to catch up extended over a prolonged period, resulting in continuous buoyancy of industrial activity, accompanied by phenomenal growth in the stock of capital. No one would deny that without the huge backlog of industrial technology made available by Western manufacturers, the Japanese could never have achieved such swift industrial recovery and continuous expansion.

It was not only the entrepreneurs who were continuously on the lookout for promising new technologies and ready to adopt them as soon as they appeared; Japanese workers and consumers were equally outward looking and bold in experimenting with new methods and new ways of industrial life. They accepted modern Western patterns of industrial life, notably mass production and mass consumption, with amazing ease. Assisted by the accommodating characteristics of company unions and the traditional practice of lifetime employment, workers were quite willing to experiment with productivity-raising mechanization and organization, since they had no fear of losing their jobs. Japanese consumers' faithful emulation of higher Western standards of consumption was clearly a key element in creating vast domestic markets for goods manufactured with imported technology and, in particular, for those marketed under well-known foreign brands.

The radically new modes of production and consumption which thus emerged revitalized Japan's industrial system. Again, this pattern is exactly what Schumpeter stressed:

. . . development consists primarily in employing existing resources in a different way, in doing new things with them irrespective of whether these resources increased or not. In the treatment of shorter epochs, moreover, this is even true in a more tangible sense. Different methods of employment, and not saving and increase in the available quantity of labor, have changed the face of the economic world in the last fifty years.[5]

Although Kenneth K. Kurihara cautioned against applying the monistic Schumpeterian theory to the intricate and complex process of Japan's postwar economic development, some of his incisive observations were clearly Schumpeterian:

The Japanese experience demonstrates, for the first time in modern economic history, the feasibility of an economy growing rapidly in spite of scarce natural resources. The permanent loss of colonial sources of raw material (that is, Korea, Formosa, Saghalien, and "Manchukuo") intensified the existing scarcity of natural resources in the defeated island nation, and yet Japan surmounted this handicap through the indigenous substitution of technological innovation, manpower utilization, and foreign trade expansion for natural resources.

Japan suffered greater devastation of material and human resources than the other vanquished nations (Germany and Italy). . . . These wartime losses did not prevent the Japanese economy from growing faster than the Germany and Italian economies, not only by augmenting the quantity of capital but, most important, through a better technical combination of available capital and labor and greater productivities of those factors.[6]

A uniquely Schumpeterian aspect of Japan's postwar economy was its method of financing investments. In Schumpeter's model, the money market serves as "the headquarters of the capitalist system" from which entrepreneurs obtain "funds of purchasing power" in the form of credit from bankers.[7] It is estimated that as much as 70 percent of postwar investment capital in Japan came from banks, while 30 percent was raised internally out of retained earnings. An inverse ratio prevails in the United States, where borrowed capital, on the average, accounts for roughly 30 percent and internal financing for the rest.[8] Predictably, such a financial method is amazing to many Western observers. For example, Robert Guillain, a noted French journalist, observed:

In order to accomplish all this [new expansion] they have poured in money so lavishly that their country now leads the world as far as investment is concerned. In some of the most advanced industries, equipment is often renewed at a rhythm that leaves Western competitors breathless; it is renewed in spite of the risk of making nearly all machinery out of date before it has been written off. Japan is poor in capital, and the problem of investment—that is to say, the finding of money to finance the continued renewal of equipment and the race for new factories—might have been a great hindrance to development. But here the country managed to overcome the difficulty by the use of the most surprising financial methods, and it is here that the extreme boldness of the managerial class is apparent. They never hesitated to run deeply into debt to set up their new installations, and they borrowed enormous sums of money from the banks. By agreeing to these loans, the banks in their turn displayed a most adventurous spirit, although it is true that it would all have come to nothing without the backing of the central bank, the Bank of Japan.*

Also implicit in the above observation is the working of what Schumpeter called "creative destruction." Many economists have noted the persistence of excess productive capacity in Japan's booming economy. Leon Hollerman, for instance, stated that according to an unpublished MITI (The Ministry of International Trade and Industry) survey, Japan's manufacturing industry was operating at 81.2 percent of its capacity in 1960 and that even in the booming year of 1964 it was producing at only 82.4 percent of capacity.[9] It is worth stressing that the nature of excess capacity in Japan was due not to a lack of aggregate demand, the usual cause of excess capacities in a stagnated economy, but in no small measure to a continuous buildup of productive capacity, which was made even at "the risk of making nearly all machinery out of date before it has been written off."[10] Thus the seemingly contradictory phenomenon of excess capacity in the booming Japanese economy reflected, at least in part, a process of creative destruction in its productive facilities; that is, a continual shift of production activity from old to newly installed and more efficient manufacturing facilities in pursuit of higher productivity.[11]

*From The Japanese Challenge by Robert Guillain, translated by Patrick O'Brian, p. 62, copyright © 1970 by J.B. Lippincott Company, reprinted by permission of the publisher.

In light of the above, Schumpeter's model fits the pattern of Japan's post-war economic development nicely; indeed, no other country in the post-war period could provide such a cogent example. Nevertheless, a word of caution is in order. Japan's experience involves a host of intricate workings of developmental processes which cannot be adequately analyzed within the broad Schumpeterian framework. The Keynesian approach is certainly needed if one wishes to examine the high rate of saving in Japan and its effect on capital formation and growth, the marginal propensity to import and the effect of economic growth on the balance of payments, the fiscal and monetary policy apparatus, and many other macroeconomic problems. Even a Marxian mode of analysis may be necessary to dramatize the problems of equity in the distribution of wealth and income, the welfare of workers, and the dual industrial structure that tends to discriminate against small-scale enterprises.[12] Equally necessary is an ecological analysis of the impact of Japan's impetuous industrial expansion on the natural environment and the quality of life.

Though Schumpeter's model is admittedly deficient in dealing with many of the detailed and intricate operations of modern Japanese economy, it does come to grips with the essential, dynamic undercurrents of Japan's industrial experience. After all, technological change and capital formation were the major catalytic agents that transformed postwar Japanese economy with such decisiveness and swiftness. Japan's economic miracle clearly resulted from technological achievement.

The Mechanism of Technological Diffusion: Product Life Cycle
It is traditional in economic analysis to treat the state of the industrial arts as a parameter of the economic system which can change only in the long run. With the acceleration of technological progress and the rapid diffusion of knowledge in modern times, a country's technological capacity may be enlarged within a surprisingly short span of time. Technological progress transforming the entire structure of an industry can occur within as little as three to five years. Indeed, this is exactly what many Japanese industries have experienced in the course of assimilating Western technology.

Licensing agreements and the overseas manufacturing operations of international corporations are the main channels of international transfers of technology. The oligopolistic market structure—a familiar feature of high-technology industries—may discourage a diffusion of industrial know-how among competing firms at home. Yet with the internationalization of their corporate operations, innovating firms may quickly transmit their latest technologies to their overseas subsidiaries and affiliates. International diffusion of technology may thus in some cases be even swifter and more effective than intracountry diffusion.

The product life cycle theory of trade is a new trade model that recognizes the quickened pace of international diffusion of technology and its effect on the pattern of trade.[13] According to this model, also known as the neotechnology account of international trade, new products catering to the demand of high-income consumers and to the labor-saving requirement of producers were first introduced in the United States, which has the highest per capita income and wage level in the world. In addition to affluent and emulative mass consumption markets that are amenable to new products and favorable to scale economies, the United States is also richly endowed with R & D resources, scientific and engineering skills, entrepreneurial and managerial talents, and above all, venture capital.[14]

Once a new product is successfully marketed in the United States, it may be exported to other countries with a similar demand structure or per capita income.[15] Thus at the initial stages of the new product's life cycle, the United States enjoys a comparative, in fact, absolute, advantage in exporting it. Later in the cycle, however, as technological difficulties are eliminated, the production process is standardized, and market acceptability develops overseas, the U.S. advantage in the new product tends to be eroded; firms in other countries which enjoy a variety of local advantages, including lower labor costs, will eventually start to produce for their own markets—and may even export later on. As a result, the United States may end up importing the very product originated in its own market.

Sensing this inevitable erosion of competitiveness, the original U.S. firm itself may foreshorten the diffusion process; it may quickly move into foreign markets through licensing agreements or foreign direct investment in an effort to retain control over its technological advantage.[16] The firm's propensity to take such an action will be stronger the more experience the firm has with overseas markets through its exporting and servicing operations, since the marginal costs of entry are already reduced.[17]

At this juncture, the product life cycle theory of trade links up to the theory of direct investment within the framework of monopolistic competition advanced by Stephen Hymer.[18] Hymer asserts that to operate successfully in a foreign market the firm must possess both a unique advantage over local firms, such as patents or differentiated products, and a strong desire to exploit such advantage.

As will be substantiated in later chapters, there is plenty of evidence that Japanese firms have actually capitalized on the product cycle sequence and the special incentives that accrue to the latecomer. Japanese followers were particularly quick in learning to reduce high initial production costs as they rapidly accumulated production and marketing experience in new products and industries under the favorable impact of their high-level economic growth. This competitive effect is discussed by Abegglen and Rapp in their approach combining the product cycle theory and the learning-by-doing hypothesis.[19] Indeed, Japanese firms have played no small part in shortening the life span of the original advantage of many U.S. firms.

By combining models of trade and investment theories, one might have predicted what actually happened next: more and more, U.S. firms became interested in setting up factories in Japan with their own capital and technology rather than licensing Japanese firms. This desire was frustrated, at least initially, by Japanese government restrictions on foreign corporate ownership. However, the recent open door policy has considerably eased controls on direct foreign investment in Japan.[20]

Chasing-Up Competition and Industrial Shedding
The phrase oiage kohka (chasing-up effect) has recently been added to the vocabulary of popular economics in Japan. It describes the effect of rising competition from developing countries on Japanese industry. As developing countries such as Taiwan, South Korea, and Singapore succeed in building light-manufacturing export industries, Japan's share of world trade in those industries will be gradually pared. Export products in which Japan's

competitiveness has already declined are cotton textiles, toys, wigs, metal tablewares, umbrellas, baseball gloves, rubber and plastic footwear, and other labor-intensive products. This trend was inevitably accentuated by recent revaluations of the Japanese yen, which eliminated the hidden price advantage of Japanese exports. To stay ahead of this unavoidable decline in traditional exports, Japan must upgrade its industrial structure by moving into more technologically sophisticated lines of industrial activity. Thus, having succeeded by means of advanced industrial know-how acquired from the West, Japan is, in turn, being chased up the ladder of industrial progress by rising competition from developing countries. Ever since Japan opened up commerce with the West in the 1860s it has demonstrated a peculiar knack for adapting to a changing world economic environment. Once again, the Japanese are demonstrating their unique adaptability in responding to the chasing-up competition from developing countries.

More and more, those segments of Japan's industry in which its comparative advantage is slipping away are being transferred to developing countries in the form of direct foreign investment. These industrial transplants are accompanied by Japanese managerial and ownership controls as well as by the transfer of production techniques and marketing skills. Because of labor shortages at home, those workers who are displaced—both currently and potentially—by the overseas migration of traditional industries can be readily absorbed into expanding, more sophisticated modern industries, with the overall result of an increase in labor productivity.

Industrial transformation at home under the pressure of the chasing-up competition is not without friction however; declining industries such as textiles, toys, and sundries are composed of many small and medium-sized enterprises. Needless to say, not all of them are interested in or capable of moving their operations into neighboring developing countries. By and large, manufacturers whose products are mainly exported opt for overseas production more readily than those whose products are mostly marketed at home, since the former are in a much better position to gain the international perspective and managerial skills required for overseas operations. After all, the export-oriented manufacturers have a stake in defending their overseas markets.

According to a recent survey, the major barriers to overseas investment for small and medium-sized enterprises are inability to communicate adequately abroad (that is, lack of knowledge of English or the local language) and unfamiliarity with local conditions.[21] In view of this, both government and private institutions provide guidance and assistance for this type of manufacturer. For example, Shokoh Chukin Bank, a semigovernmental bank designed to assist small and medium-sized enterprises, is active in providing advice and loans to firms interested in overseas ventures. With the encouragement of MITI all the major city branches of the Japan Chamber of Commerce have set up a free consultation program and technical assistance for overseas investment. The Institute of Developing Economies (formerly, the Institute of Asian Economic Affairs) also provides information on investment environments in Asian countries.

But perhaps the most practical and effective help is offered by Japan's powerful trading companies, which have themselves become active participants in multinational operations. Until recently, trading firms engaged in, and profited from, assisting Japanese manufacturers in domestic as well as overseas trade. In 1968, for example, their share of Japan's foreign trade was 48.2 percent in exports and 63.1 percent in imports.[22]

Although their go-between role in international trade is still significant and is even expanding in third-country trade involving the exports of less-developed countries that lack marketing ability, the trading companies are no longer content to operate as commission brokers. Instead, they are actively investing in overseas ventures that offer new opportunities for longer-term profits; they can serve as intermediaries, on a continuous basis, for the exports of required machinery, equipment, and unfinished products from Japan to their overseas ventures, and for the marketing of their overseas output in both local and export markets.[23] Moreover, they can share in the long run growth of the overseas investments in which they participate.

The strength of the trading companies lies in their worldwide network of marketing facilities, well staffed with experts trained in local languages and experienced in negotiating with local authorities and business interests. They can offer not only managerial and marketing skills but also strong financial backup. Their services are particularly attractive to small and medium-sized enterprises interested in overseas operations.

In developing countries, therefore, many Japanese ventures exhibit the following pattern of capital ownership: about 50 percent of the total capital is locally owned, 20–30 percent is owned by the Japanese manufacturer involved, and the balance is financed by a trading company. The trading companies' share of capital ownership in manufacturing ventures is generally much larger in advanced countries where foreign capital ownership is less restricted and risks are much lower.[24]

Despite all the assistance rendered to this type of company, there are still a large number of small and medium-sized manufacturers of traditional products which are desperately struggling to remain competitive at home. Although their economic power has been weakened, they still retain a political clout. As a result, Japan's preferential tariff program for imports from developing countries, which was initiated on August 1, 1971, under the pressure exerted by the UNCTAD conferences, is largely a political gesture to lend an ear to the aspiration of developing countries to earn foreign exchange through "trade, not aid." It is expected that, at least for a time, the government will be slow in opening up domestic markets for imports directly competitive with declining industries. The future schedule of Japan's tariff preference program is likely to be synchronized with its effort to modernize domestic industries with the minimum possible disturbance to those firms still remaining in the declining sector.

In the meantime, small and medium-sized firms threatened by competition from developing countries will be assisted to move their production to labor-abundant countries. Thus Japan's manufacturing investments in developing countries may be increasingly designed to partake of the benefits of its own preferential tariffs conferred on developing countries. This is an interesting, and perhaps efficient, variant of adjustment assistance to import-injured firms.[25]

Some developing countries, such as South Korea and Taiwan, are outgrowing the stage of development which depends on light-manufacturing industries and beginning to emphasize the development of heavy and chemical industries. But the Japanese economy is not as much threatened by this new development as it might have been only a few years ago. The transition of economic development in Japan's neighbor countries is taking place at a most opportune time; Japan now wants to shed some of its heavy and chemical industries, and is quite willing to transfer them to neighboring countries, particularly those industries whose further development at home entails high ecological costs.

Although Japan's postwar economic policy of emphasizing large-scale heavy and chemical industries has been impressively successful, it has had a host of undesirable effects both at home and overseas. In the first place, since Japan is a small island nation, the supply of industrial sites has quickly diminished, and the problem of pollution caused by high levels of production and consumption has nearly reached the level of a public health hazard. The labor supply, particularly of factory workers, has become extremely scarce, causing wage rates to rise phenomenally.

On the trade front, the upsurge in Japan's exports to foreign countries, especially to the United States, was met there by a loud clamor for protection by local industries. Industrial expansion centered in heavy and chemical industries has been accompanied by rising import dependence on the foreign supply of natural resources, which has meant increased vulnerability of the Japanese economy as well as a potential source of conflict with other resource-importing industrial countries.

The rapidly rising social costs of industrial expansion at home have finally forced Japan to reexamine its postwar industrial policy. A recently emerged consumerism has also added fuel to the dissatisfaction of the people with the postwar pursuit of GNP growthmanship, carried out as it was at the cost of deterioration of their living environment.

It was against this background that the Japanese government, in its 1971 White Paper on International Trade and Industry, announced an epoch-making policy for the economy to follow in the future. The new policy emphasizes a reorientation of the economy away from "pollution-prone" and "natural-resource-consuming" heavy and chemical industries and toward "clean" and "brain-intensive" industries. On the international front, it stresses a greater reliance than before on exports which compete in quality, variety, and sophisticated design rather than in price.

These housecleaning operations imply an encouragement of the migration not only of labor-intensive conventional industries but also of heavy and chemical industries. MITI is reportedly working on a blueprint to alter the industrial structure with special taxes and other fiscal measures.[26]

Sensing this new trend, some developing countries are showing eagerness to attract Japan's fading industries such as the manufacture of metal castings, bicycles, sewing machines, telescopes, ceramics, leather products, and the like. South Korea, in particular, appears interested in strengthening labor-intensive industries such as these, so that with its relatively cheap but efficient manpower, it can develop export competitiveness.[27] This type of industrial transfer may, however, be a temporary phenomenon, as the developing countries eventually stress the development of more sophisticated industries.

Japan also is extending assistance to heavy industries; for example, it is helping establish an integrated steel complex in South Korea—a project that only a few years before had been judged premature for the Korean economy and turned down by a consortium of U.S. and European companies. Admittedly, the Korean project might have been influenced by political considerations rather than by the recently announced policy consideration. But MITI is reportedly considering the possibility of a regional industrial-development plan which envisages the establishment of heavy and chemical industries, specifically steel and petrochemicals, in other Asian countries.[28]

The shipbuilding industry, Japan's star export industry, has been active recently in assisting developing countries to build shipyards. Ishikawajima-Harima Heavy Industries Co., which already has shipyards under joint venture with the local governments in Brazil and Singapore, is going to set up another joint venture in Turkey. Other major shipyards, such as Mitsubishi, Sumitomo, and Kawasaki, are also in the stage of negotiation with developing countries. Although they are diluting their own competitiveness by fostering foreign builders, the sale of a variety of machinery and equipment that their diversified shipyards can produce is being encouraged.

Besides, since shipbuilding is a highly labor-intensive industry, Japan may eventually lose its hegemony to labor-abundant developing countries. Joint ventures overseas will at least ensure partial control and long-run profits.

Outflows of direct investment capital to other advanced countries whose markets have hitherto been served mainly by exports are growing likewise. Rising protectionism in the United States and Europe as a reaction to Japan's lopsided trade surpluses has necessitated a switch of Japanese manufacturers' strategy from exports to either local production or third-country production.[29]

In sum, Japan is in the midst of industrial reorganization, shedding and transferring to developing countries those segments of its industry in which it is losing comparative advantages or can no longer expand because of domestic problems of congestion and pollution resulting from the high density of industrial concentration. Japan also is shifting from exports to production in Western countries themselves. No doubt the recent revaluations of the yen boosted both its interest in investing overseas and its capacity to do so, since the revaluations eliminated its export price advantage and since Japanese firms were able to make investments overseas in appreciated currency. Indeed, one may even argue that the appreciation of the yen, which was forced upon Japan by the successive devaluations of the U.S. dollar, occurred at a most opportune time, since many Japanese industries had already reached a physical limit of expansion at home and many of their exports had captured overseas markets to such an extent that any further expansion was politically undesirable in local markets. As the undervalued yen and the relatively free trade policy of the West, particularly of the United States, helped Japan's exports in the past, so may the revalued yen and the open-arm welcome extended presently by the United States to the inflow of Japanese capital assist Japan's new economic penetration of the U.S. market.

Needless to say, whether Japan can continue to renovate the industrial structure to its advantage remains to be seen. Future political and social developments both at home and overseas are unseen constraints on the momentum of Japan's industrial progress, which is now in the new stage of overseas expansion.

The Economic Action of Challenge and Response: Adaptive Dynamism
As a middle-advanced country in terms of per capita income and living
standard, Japan finds itself in a psychologically ambivalent situation; it
has a deep-seated inferiority complex; it admires the West, but at the same
time it feels superior to neighboring Asian countries. This very ambiv-
alence, however, provides a double-pronged challenge to the Japanese. The
West has long been, and still is, a paragon of modernity and industrialization, a model that the Japanese wish to emulate. On the other hand, their
pride in being the only truly industrialized country in Asia is an equally
powerful motive for them to continue to advance lest they be overtaken
by neighboring countries.

Japan's tactic has been to chart carefully its modernization as coordinated
responses to challenges—opportunities or threats—in the world economic
environment. As Arnold J. Toynbee has emphasized, what counts in the
formation of a civilization is the reaction of a nation to external stimuli,
adversities encountered on the path of its endeavors, and not the weight of
the inanimate objects of its environment.[30] Indeed, it is futile to try to
explain Japan's industrial progress and its trade competitiveness in terms of
its domestic economic environment, which is characterized by an exiguity
of natural resources and by frequent natural hazards such as typhoons,
earthquakes, and tidal waves. In fact, any attempt to find a reason for
Japan's economic success in its physical make-up only reaffirms its mys-
tique as an economic miracle.

The secrets of Japan's success lie in its capacity to react to adverse conditions in positive ways and turn them into advantages. For example, a
limited supply of industrial sites led the Japanese to reclaim coastal areas
to create many ideal polders for steelworks and petrochemical plants. They
proved to be extremely efficient in handling bulky raw materials and trans-
porting finished outputs by ocean routes. On the trade front, Japan has
shown equally remarkable foresight and adaptability, building productive
capacities in those industrial sectors where the world's demands have rapidly been expanding. Its export expansion in automobiles (some with
rotary engines), huge oil tankers, motorcycles, transistor radios, miniature
TV sets, desk-top calculators, and the like has been the result of entrepreneurial and technological adaptability—and in fact, of little else.

The conventional factor endowments theory of trade throws little light on the adaptive dynamism of the Japanese economy. To be sure, Japan has a relatively abundant, highly skilled and disciplined labor force suitable for mass-producing modern products; this is no doubt a factor in its comparative advantage. But a more fundamental question that should be asked is, How has Japan come to develop export competitiveness in, say, technology-based products?[31] The factor endowments theory is essentially static and cross sectional in analysis; it can only broadly illuminate the pattern of trade at a given point in time, but it cannot by itself explain or predict the creation and demise of a country's comparative advantage, particularly in a technology-based manufacture.

In this respect, an eclectic approach combining the product cycle theory, the learning-by-doing theory and the analysis of the effect of the chasing-up competition seems to provide a more appropriate framework for understanding Japan's dynamic trade competitiveness. For Japan's export strength lies in adroitly maneuvering in the changing world economic environment.

The revaluation of yen, forced on Japan by the successive devaluations of the U.S. dollar, has already proved to be a benefit for Japan as its industry expands overseas through direct investment. Even the Middle East oil crisis may be turned to advantage in the long run. As we see in Chapter 5, Japan has started earnestly to develop alternative energy resources, such as solar and geothermal energy, by stepping up research efforts. In addition, because of the oil crisis, Japan's efforts to develop independent oil sources will not create as much friction with Western oil interests as they would have in the past. Japan's economic ties with Arab nations will inevitably be strengthened as it eagerly provides industrial and technological assistance for the economic development of the Arab world in return for an assured supply of oil on which Japan is currently so dependent. As a result, Japanese industry will very likely gain strong footholds in the rich Arab markets.

As Charles P. Kindleberger succinctly puts it, "The world of foreign trade is one of change. It makes a great difference to the trade of different countries, and to the impact of trade on them, whether they are capable of changing with the world."[32]

2 Acquisition of Foreign Technology

Postwar Program of Technology Imports

Japan has succeeded in casting off the old stigma of being an exporter of shoddy manufactures and is now gaining a worldwide reputation as a manufacturer of high-quality products. Indeed, Japan's postwar economic expansion was essentially spurred by its effort to catch up with the West in the industrial arts. To cite a typical observation:

Hailed sometimes as a "miracle," there is nothing mysterious about Japan's high-pitched growth. The factors immediately at work are well known . . . the principal gain . . . has come from a sustained rise in the productivity of labor. . . . A key impulse to this productivity gain has come from the great wave of technical borrowing from abroad since the occupation. The isolation and destruction of the war had caused Japan to lag well behind the West in the industrial arts. As soon as possible her businessmen and public agencies moved energetically to repair the gap, importing the latest technologies over a wide front to rebuild their industrial plant.[1]

How did the Japanese acquire advanced Western technologies? What were the nature and scope of technologies imported? Fortunately, there is plenty of detailed information to analyze these questions since the Japanese government has kept, by way of its controls, a complete track of foreign technologies acquired. All Japanese firms' purchases of foreign know-how require government approval under the Foreign Investment Law, and the remittances of royalties and fees are subject to the foreign exchange regulations.

The Foreign Exchange and Foreign Trade Control Law—generally known as the Foreign Exchange Control Law—was enacted in 1949 for the purpose of regulating the use of foreign exchange reserves that were in short supply in the early postwar period. Under this law, all the external transactions involving remittances in foreign currency had to be approved by the government. On the other hand, the Foreign Investment Law—formally, the Law Concerning Foreign Investment—legislated in 1950 was intended to promote an inflow of foreign capital and technology in order to develop the Japanese economy and to improve its international payments position. The Foreign Investment Law takes a positive approach to enhance the economy's capacity to earn foreign exchange by fostering both import-competing and export industries at home. This feature is in contrast with the passive nature of the Foreign Exchange Control Law that was designed to ration available foreign exchange reserves.

The positive nature of the Foreign Investment Law is clearly set forth in its preamble:

The purpose of this law is to create a sound basis for foreign investment in Japan, by limiting the induction of foreign investment to that which will contribute to the self-support and sound development of the Japanese economy and to the improvement of the international balance of payments; by providing for remittances arising from foreign investment, and by providing for adequate protection for such investment.[2]

Two phrases in the above preamble are worth our special attention. The phrase "limiting the induction of foreign investment to that which will contribute to the self-support and sound development of the Japanese economy" seems to imply that without appropriate government controls, the acquisition of the foreign capital and technology will lead to the domination of the Japanese economy by foreign interests. Indeed, as will be discussed in Chapter 4, this is the basic assumption held by the government in formulating its policy for the acquisition of foreign capital and technology.

The phrase "providing for remittances arising from foreign investment" relates to the government's intention to provide a full guarantee of the repatriation of earnings once the investment project is approved. Although the fundamental objective of the law was to build up domestic industries with the help of foreign capital and technology—but without being dominated by foreign interests—the guaranteed remittances of investment earnings were emphasized as a primary justification of the controls. For instance, this attitude was reflected in a speech made by the then Prime Minister Hayato Ikeda in New York City in 1950:

As to the first point of assuring transfer, our dollar position does not allow us to serve every Tom, Dick and Harry and let them exchange their yen earnings and take dollars home. We are bound to be selective in this respect. Of course, everybody is welcomed in so far as he does not demand a prior commitment of the Government for transfer. It is however, much more advisable that he tells the Government beforehand about his investment and sees how much the Government guarantees to transfer out of the profit. The rate of the transfer will be different according to the merit of the proposed investment. When the Government commits itself to a certain amount of transfer, the Government is legally obligated to incorporate the commitment in its running dollar budget. Then there will be no default. This checking system is by no means intended to create red tape.

It is a device of a poor but honest borrower who does not want to cheat creditors. The related law clearly states that these checkings and restrictions will be removed one by one as our dollar position warrants the removal.[3]

There was, no doubt, a genuine concern on the part of the Japanese government that one be an "honest borrower." As Ikeda promised, the government did gradually reduce its restrictions on the inflow of foreign capital and technology as well as the remittance of profits as Japan's foreign reserve position improved.

Japan's imports of technology over the period of 1950–1971 are shown in Figure 2.1. The numbers represent a complete enumeration of technology purchase contracts approved in each year under the Foreign Investment Law. Category A comprises those contracts that have an effective life of more than one year with the payment of royalties guaranteed to be made in foreign currency. Category B, on the other hand, covers those contracts that call for royalty payments in the Japanese yen or have an effective life of less than a year. The latter normally includes incidental arrangements such as an invitation of foreign engineers or an acquisition of drawings.

It is interesting to note that technology imports of category B started to decline in 1968. This may signal a turning point in Japan's postwar technological progress; its technical capacity had substantially advanced to such an extent that industry became less dependent on incidental technical assistance from the West. On the other hand, it also may indicate the fact that subsequent upon a major technology import liberalization implemented in 1968, relatively insignificant technologies began to be imported under category A with the result of a decline in the purchase of supplementary technical assistance.

Needless to say, the inflow of Western know-how into Japan has not been limited to this government-controlled channel of technology contracts. Technological progress was equally assisted, indirectly, through the import of capital goods embodying advanced technology, the education of scientists and engineers in the West, or simply through the study of foreign technical literature. Yet significant industrial techniques, whether patented or unpatented, were as a rule imparted by Western firms only under special

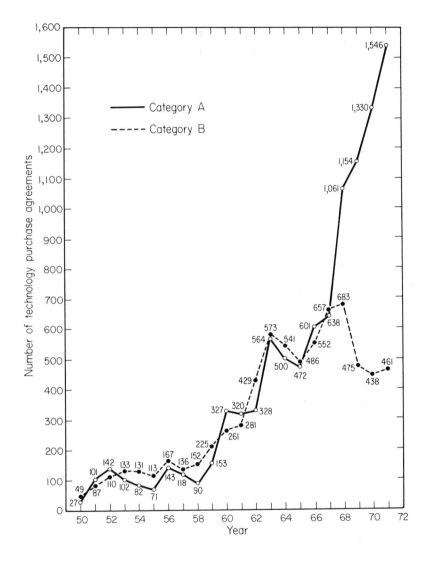

Figure 2.1. Technology imports—number of contracts for the purchase of technology, categories A and B, 1950-1971

arrangements such as licensing agreements, joint venture contracts, and subsidiary operations. These arrangements required official approval if the repatriation of earnings was to be guaranteed.

Gradual improvements in Japan's foreign reserve position were concomitant to the recovery and expansion of its economy which were greatly accelerated by the successful absorption of foreign technologies. Throughout the postwar period Japan endeavored to reorient its industrial structure from light manufacturing toward heavy and chemical industries. This structural transformation was assisted by various fiscal measures, including tax benefits, accelerated depreciation and special allocations of foreign exchange for the importation of machinery, equipment, and raw materials. The acquisition of foreign technology was also an essential instrument for facilitating the transformation. In fact, the government directed the inflow of foreign technologies by making announcements as to what types of technology were desired for the economy.[4] Two lists of such announcements made in 1950 and 1959 are shown in Table 2.1.

It is of interest to note that the first list covered only those technologies that were essential for introducing new producer goods and processes in existing industries; on the other hand, the second list, reflecting Japan's further effort to move its industry toward more sophisticated levels of activity, was aimed at fostering new sectors such as jet aircraft and electronic products and increasing productive efficiency with the introduction of assembly lines and automated processes.

Another interesting feature of Japan's technology import program was that Japanese firms seeking official approval for technology purchases were required to give a statement on the possible economic benefits to themselves and the anticipated effect of imported technology upon the economy; they were forced to consider both their private and national interests.

Gradual Liberalization
With the unexpectedly quick recovery and strengthening of the economy and its balance of payments position, government restrictions began to be gradually removed. The first major relaxation was made in July 1959. The scope of approval was extended to allow the acquisition of less significant

Table 2.1. Announcement of Desired Technological Assistance.
Selected Processes and other Technological Assistance

A. 1950

Textiles
1. Acetate flake and fibers
2. Other synthetic fibers

Chemicals
1. Granulation of calcium cyanamide and calcium phosphate fertilizer
2. Synthetic phenol
3. Vinyl chloride
4. Melamin resins
5. Silicon resins
6. Pigments
7. Furnace black

Petroleum
1. Lubricants by solvent refining method
2. Catalytic cracking and cracked olefin gas
3. Addition agents to lubricants

Ceramic products
1. Furnace bed materials

Metals
1. Soaking pit, reheating furnace and annealing furnace for steel making

Mining
1. Coal preparation

Pharmaceuticals
1. Streptomycin
2. Chloromycetin
3. Aureomycin

Nonelectrical Machinery
1. Continuous welded pipe drawing
2. Continuous wire drawing
3. Continuous spinning machinery
4. Gyro-compass for marine use
5. Dynamic pressure log for marine use
6. Welding of ship's hulls

Electrical Machinery
1. 1-50 type integrating wall-hour meters
2. Demand meters
3. Monopole type mercury rectifiers
4. Plastic insulated wires and cables
5. Power and tele-communication cables
6. Frequency modulation system in radio communication
7. Hyperbolic marine radio navigation system
8. Microwave vacuum tubes
9. G.T. tubes and M.T. tubes
10. X-ray tubes of revolving anode type

B. 1959

Chemicals
Chemical products from natural gas or petroleum gas

Metals
Heat-proof alloys and steel

Nonelectrical Machinery
Highly efficient machine tools

Electrical Machinery Industry
Electronics

Aircraft
Jet aircraft (including engines and engine accessories)

Industries in General
Techniques making processes continuous, more efficient or automated

Sources: The 1950 list adopted from Japanese Ministry of International Trade and Industry, The Announcement of Desired Technological Assistance (Tokyo: 1950); and the 1959 list from OECD, Liberalization of International Capital Movements—Japan (Paris: 1968), pp. 49–50.

technologies, including those related to the production of consumer goods. Guaranteed remittances, however, were left subject to the proviso of a temporary suspension in the event of an adverse balance of payments condition.

In 1960 there was a shift from the so-called "positive" to a "negative" screening standard. Under the new system, technology purchase contracts were approved so long as they were judged not to cause any detrimental effects on the economy; previously, they were approved only on the basis of their "positive" contributions to the economy.

When Japan became an Article 8 country of IMF (the International Monetary Fund) and a member country of OECD (the Organization for Economic Cooperation and Development) in 1964, restrictions were further lifted, and approval procedures were simplified.

It was not until 1968, however, that a full scale of technology import liberalization took place. In that year all technology purchase contracts with compensations less than $50,000 in each case for sectors other than those specifically restricted by the government (that is, aircraft, weapons, explosives, nuclear energy, space exploration, computers and petrochemicals), began to be approved automatically by the Bank of Japan unless the government filed an injunction no later than one month after application.

The secular upward trend of technological imports depicted in Figure 2.1 closely mirrors the above gradual steps for liberalization taken by the government. As former Prime Minister Ikeda promised in 1950, decontrols were indeed implemented with the improvement of Japan's capacity to earn foreign exchange. Needless to say, this in turn was a result of economic development.

In this connection it is interesting to look at Japan's economic growth rates, international reserves, and technology imports (category A) over the period of 1950–1970 which are shown in Table 2.2. Secular upward trends in the three variables no doubt reflect mutually reinforcing interactions among them; technology imports contributed to Japan's economic growth and its capacity to earn foreign exchange through exports; improved inter-

Table 2.2. Economic Growth Rate, International Reserves, and Technology Imports (Category A), 1950–1970

	GNP Growth rate (real)[a]	International official reserves[b] (in millions of dollars)	Technology imports (category A)[a]
1950		564	27
1951		924	101
1952	13.0	979	142
1953	7.9	823	102
1954	2.3	738	82
1955	11.4	768	71
1956	6.8	941	143
1957	8.3	524	118
1958	5.7	861	90
1959	11.7	1,322	153
1960	13.3	1,824	327
1961	14.4	1,486	320
1962	5.7	1,841	328
1963	12.8	1,878	564
1964	10.4	1,999	500
1965	5.4	2,107	472
1966	14.4	2,074	601
1967	13.1	2,005	638
1968	13.7	2,891	1,061
1969	12.6	3,496	1,154
1970	10.3	4,399	1,330

Sources: GNP growth rate and international official reserves are from the Bank of Japan, Economic Statistics Annual (Tokyo: The Bank of Japan, 1967 and 1972); and technology imports from Japanese Science and Technology Agency, 1970–Gaikoku Gijutsu Dohnyu Nenji Hohkoku [1970–Annual Report on Absorption of Foreign Technology] (Tokyo: Printing Office, The Ministry of Finance, 1972).

[a]Fiscal year

[b]Year-end

national reserve position led to the decontrols of technology imports, which in turn stimulated economic expansion and exports. Empirical evidence for this phenomenon is presented in Chapter 3.

Note also similar patterns of fluctuations; slowdowns in economic growth were generally accompanied by declines both in foreign exchange reserves and the volume of technology imports—whenever the economy was confronted with any balance of payments difficulty, the government applied deflationary policy to cool down the heated expansion of industry and also made the screening of technology imports more stringent. This relationship was particularly discernible during the 1950s when Japan's reserve position was precarious. Indeed, twice during the 1950s—namely, in 1953–1954 and in 1958–1959—an adverse reserve position led to a recession and a decline in the number of technology imports approved.[5]

With the advent of the sixties, however, Japan's reserve position began to improve considerably, and technology imports were substantially liberalized. As a result, technology imports declined only in the 1965 recession that affected adversely businessmen's expectations—despite a comfortable size of international reserves.

There were some major characteristic differences between the technologies imported during the 1950s and those during the 1960s. During the first decade the producer goods sector was the principal buyer of foreign technology, whereas during the second decade the consumer goods sector also was permitted increasingly to import technical know-how, much of which was relatively insignificant—some were nothing but brand names. It may therefore be generalized that the technologies imported during the 1950s had in large measure a growth-inducing impact on the economy as they directly contributed to the buildup of productive capacity; while those imported during the 1960s were in many cases induced by Japan's economic growth itself, and so may be characterized as growth-induced.

Favorable Supply Conditions
When the government-controlled import program of technology was initiated in 1950, there was less danger of foreign domination of industries than some economic planners and businessmen had feared. In the early 1950s—that is, prior to a boom touched off by U.S. procurement during the Korean War—the Japanese economy was still prostrate without any sign of economic recovery attractive enough for foreign investors. U.S. firms, in particular, were at that time more interested in the growing European economies. It was, therefore, the Japanese who played an initiatory role in negotiating technology contracts, and most Western firms, not especially attracted by Japanese markets, were willing to supply technology primarily through licensing.

There were, nevertheless, some firms that were reluctant to license their technologies because of the fear of nurturing future competition. One American firm explains that "it has no intention of teaching a licensee what the licensee needs to become a well-equipped competitor in a few years."[6] In fact, there is evidence that the Japanese at times encountered supply difficulties. In the mid-fifties, for example, Swiss and West German manufacturers of high-grade precision tools were reluctant to provide the technology to the Japanese machine tool industry as they feared potential competition.[7]

The Japanese were, however, eventually successful in one way or another in finding the sellers of desired technologies. One of the factors favoring Japan as a buyer was the availability of alternative sources of supply. If the Japanese could not secure a given type of technology from, say, British firms, they managed to find alternative suppliers in other countries. This is partly evidenced in a report of a British business group that visited Japan in the early sixties:

It is only during the past three or four years, during which over 1,000 more technical agreements have been arranged, that British manufacturers have appreciated the wisdom of selling "know-how" to Japan (in the knowledge that if they do not, others are willing to) and the number of Anglo-Japanese technical agreements have risen to around 150 and there are many others known to be in the pipeline.[8]

A similar story is likely to be told by businessmen in other countries.

The nationalities of suppliers of technology (category A) to Japan are shown in Table 2.3. The United States is the major supplier, accounting for as much as 57.8 percent of the total contracts concluded during the period of 1950–1970, although there was a decline in the U.S. share in the 1960s compared with the 1950s—an indication of a narrowing technology gap between the United States and the rest of the world. The U.S. share is actually somewhat greater since the suppliers in such countries as Liechtenstein, Switzerland and Panama include many U.S. subsidiaries. Without doubt, the United States played no small part in making other Western countries appreciate "the wisdom of selling 'know-how' to Japan."

One may wonder why U.S. firms have been so generous in supplying technology to aggressive Japanese firms. There are many possible reasons. For

Table 2.3. Supply of Technology by Country: (1950–1970)

Country	1950–1959		1960–1970		Total	
	Number	Percentage	Number	Percentage	Number	Percentage
United States	665	64.6%	4,144	56.8%	4,809	57.8%
Canada	24	2.3	115	1.6	139	1.7
United Kingdom	34	3.3	589	8.1	623	7.5
West Germany	71	6.9	930	12.7	1,001	12.0
France	34	3.3	318	4.4	352	4.2
Switzerland	81	7.9	439	6.0	520	6.2
Italy	25	2.4	124	1.7	149	1.8
Holland	31	3.0	187	2.6	218	2.6
Belgium	1	0.1	43	0.6	44	0.5
Denmark	6	0.6	51	0.7	57	0.7
Sweden	21	2.0	90	1.2	111	1.3
Australia	2	0.2	27	0.4	30	0.4
Soviet Union	0	0	18	0.3	18	0.2
Other	34	3.3	220	3.0	253	3.0
Total	1,029	100.0	7,295	100.0	8,324	100.0

Source: Japanese Science and Technology Agency, 1970–Gaikoku Gijutsu Dohnyu Nenji Hohkoku [1970–Annual Report on Absorption of Foreign Technology] (Tokyo: Printing Office, The Ministry of Finance, 1972).

example, Albert O. Hirschman points out that, in contrast to the industrial countries of Europe, particularly Britain and Germany, which "viewed with concern and alarm the building of foreign industries," the United States has been less concerned about imparting industrial knowledge and helping other countries to industrialize; besides, U.S. exports are, on the whole, geared to high and expanding levels of income, and the United States is less dependent on foreign sources of supply that might be cut off by industrialization abroad.[9]

Equally important is, however, the fact that there is perhaps much stronger interfirm competition in the United States for improving existing products and marketing new ones than in any other Western country. This point has been stressed earlier in our discussion of the product cycle theory of trade; high-income products and labor-saving devices are introduced one after another in the U.S. markets.[10] High levels of R & D activity in technology-based industries entail not only "internally-induced" obsolescences of existing products and processes (that is, technical progress within a firm) but also "externally-induced" obsolescences (that is, technological competition between firms). If the firm is in the vanguard of technological progress, there is little reason to fear fostering competition. For example, an aircraft company's executive is quoted as stating that "[his company] feels relatively secure in releasing current know-how to licensees, because of [his company's] greatly superior research facilities and the rapid rate of technological change and new product development in the industry."[11]

In the face of fierce interfirm technological competition, any individual firm's effort to jealously guard its industrial arts would be of a temporary duration. Other firms are most likely to make available similar or even superior technology. If existing technology is, therefore, doomed to have a short life expectancy, there is an added incentive to sell it to those who can make the best use of it and, hence, can pay the largest possible amount of royalties. In this regard, aggressive Japanese firms have proved to be the best users of U.S. technologies. Viewed in this light, the combined forces of interfirm competition and a rapid rate of intrafirm technological progress appear to have been a greater inducement for U.S. firms to transfer industrial know-how than the forces of intercountry competition.

The fact that Japan was the number one customer for U.S. technologies in the postwar period is partly evidenced in an OECD study presented in Table 2.4. It shows that in the early 1960s the United States received the largest sum of royalty payments from Japan among the five major importers of U.S. patents and licenses. Although no comparable data are available for more recent years, Japan's leading position as a user of U.S. technology is most likely to have expanded. For Japan's phenomenal economic growth must have accompanied a rise in royalty payments, which are closely tied to the sales of the goods and services produced with imported technology.

The willingness of U.S. firms to impart industrial knowledge to foreign firms also may be rooted in the development-centered pattern of their R & D efforts. United States firms' strength in commercial applications of inventions is well known. It is often said that many major inventions were originated in Europe but were commercialized in the United States. Development is usually more expensive than basic research, often running two to three times (or even more) as much.[12] Large U.S. firms, in which the R & D activity of the United States is heavily concentrated, have financial capacity as well as the affluent home markets which are conducive to commercialization of new inventions. Federally supported R & D activity in aerospace and defense, moreover, produces numerous technological spin-offs for commercial application.

Development effort is quite different in nature from basic research, as Daniel Hamberg observes:

No derogation of the importance of the development stage is intended when we say that typically it involves a much lower order of inventive activity than research does; in fact, it involves little or no inventive activity. It often calls for great technical skill, engineering knowledge, and much resourcefulness. But it is not creative, or is so only to a minimal extent. Its task is essentially one of adaptation to or within known methods of production. The types and levels of talent required in development are thus distinctly inferior to those required to perform original and creative research and invention.[13]

The results of such "less creative" efforts are in many cases unpatentable, though commercially valuable, and consequently highly susceptible to being copied by competitors. As a result, U.S. firms might have been motivated to license technical know-how to potential imitators. In this

Table 2.4 United States Receipts from Technology Exports (Patents, Licenses and Technological Know-how)[a] (in millions of U.S. dollars)

Japan (1963)	84.7
United Kingdom (1964)	81.8
Germany (1964)	65.3
France (1963)	59.7
Italy (1963)	57.2
Total receipts from the above countries	348.7
Total receipts from all countries	550.0
As percentage of total receipts of the above 5 countries	67.2

Source: Adopted from Table 9 in OECD, Gaps in Technology: Analytical Report, (Paris: 1970) p. 201.

[a]Excluding management fees and service charges

way, any unpatentable technical information may be legally protected under licensing contracts.

Another reason for U.S. firms' magnanimous attitude for supplying technology to Japan during the 1950s, if not in the 1960s, was that they viewed royalties as windfall gains and did not consider Japanese manufacturers seriously as their competitors:

A review of the history of Japanese acquisition of foreign technology, and its impact on competitive relations in world markets, can only lead to the conclusion that much of the sale of technology to Japan·has been short-sighted and ill-advised from the point of view of the Western licensor. It is quite clear that royalty payments on significant developments need to be very high indeed to compensate fully for the very high costs of development. Yet there has been a tendency to view payments for technology as windfall income, and to make little effort to determine a fair price.[14]

All in all, moreover, U.S. firms are favorably disposed to international business opportunities, as evidenced by the rapidly expanding overseas operations of U.S.-based multinational corporations. This outgoing attribute of U.S. business, fostered by economic factors such as the availability of surplus capital, high and ever-rising labor costs at home, and trade barriers set up by other countries is certainly responsible for technology outflow. The United States appears to be well on the way to becoming a "mature creditor" economy with its productive facilities increasingly transferred overseas.[15]

The U.S. government's postwar foreign policy also contributed significantly to the relatively unrestricted mode of technology outflows from the United States to its allies in particular and to the rest of the world in general—except the Communist countries. Although no policy on technology trade as such existed, the U.S. government treated international movements of capital and technology as part of its freer trade policy and left them largely to the dictates of market forces.[16]

3 Technological Assimilation, Trade Performance, and Capital Formation in the Fifties

We have seen in Chapter 2 that the Japanese government initially made it a policy to approve only those technology purchase contracts that would be, in its judgment, instrumental in either developing key industries or improving Japan's trade position. Such a selection policy, if successful, would result in the buildup of key industries and the strengthening of Japan's trade competitiveness both through export expansion and import substitution. Indeed, there is plenty of evidence that the government has largely accomplished such policy objectives. In this chapter we take a look at some of the telling evidence of this successful program.

Export Competitiveness

The shares of selected industrial countries in world export markets are shown in Table 3.1. Japan's share multiplied nearly threefold between 1955 and 1970, advancing from eighth to third position among the 10 leading industrial countries. On the other hand, the share of the United States, and that of the United Kingdom in particular, declined drastically.

A country's export strength as reflected in its market share is affected by demand and supply conditions both at home and abroad. Equally important are the commercial policies pursued by the governments of trading

Table 3.1. Export Shares of Selected Industrial Countries in World Markets in 1955 and 1970 (in percentage)[a]

Country	1955	1970
Japan	2.4	6.9
Canada	5.7	6.0
United States	18.5	15.5
The Netherlands	3.2	4.2
West Germany	7.4	12.2
France	5.8	6.4
Italy	2.2	4.7
United Kingdom	10.0	6.9
Sweden	2.1	2.4
Denmark	1.3	1.2

Source: Japanese Ministry of International Trade and Industry, 1972–Tsushoh Hakusho, [1972–White Paper on International Trade] (Tokyo: MITI, 1972).

[a]As a percentage of the world's exports, excluding those of the Communist countries.

countries. All these demand, supply, and policy factors interact among themselves in a set of complex matrices, intensifying or neutralizing each other's effect on the country's trade performance.

There are two types of changes in the supply of exports which are particularly worth noting; one which is induced by conditions inside the country and the other caused by conditions outside the country. For example, exports are affected by any production adjustment required in catering to changing domestic markets—but only in such a passive manner as a residual from domestic economic activities.[1] This type of induced change in the supply of exports occurs in large economies with a relatively small trade dependence, such as the United States. On the other hand, manufacturers in export-oriented countries such as Japan are constantly scanning overseas markets for sales opportunities; their product innovations are closely geared to the incomes and tastes of advanced overseas markets rather than to those of their own domestic markets. For instance, the export production of transistorized FM radios in Japan, which are identified as a significant Japanese innovation by an OECD study,[2] occurred prior to the domestic FM broadcasting.[3]

There are many other examples of these types of products that were initially produced solely for export and later marketed at home. Such a tendency is particularly strong in Japanese industries since they have been involved as aggressive absorbers of new Western technologies, as discussed in connection with the product cycle theory of trade in Chapter 1. Thus it was often domestic trade that turned out to be a residual or an extension of export activities—rather than the other way around.[4] Of course, this phenomenon is nothing new in the history of world trade. Perhaps the best known case is Swiss export of watches.[5] A small country can avail itself of outside markets, reaping the benefits of scale economies, and building up its domestic sector as an extension of advanced foreign markets.

It is also worth stressing here that the strong orientation of Japan's consumer goods industries to the high-income markets of Western countries was in complete harmony with the domestic market inasmuch as Japanese consumers on the whole are avid followers of the tastes and consumption patterns of Western countries. In this respect, the consumption pattern of the American people played a particularly important role as a standard for the Japanese to emulate. Indeed, Japan's economic growth has been largely synonymous with the Americanization of consumer tastes in Japan. Any consumer product that had been successfully exported to the United States was readily accepted later in the domestic market.[6]

Competitive Factors

In Western countries Japan's exports, standardized products as represented by cotton textiles, toys, and sundries, were traditionally regarded as low-technology products, which were able to compete only in price. In fact, the label "made-in-Japan" was looked upon as a sign of cheapness—poor quality and low price. In the postwar period, however, this image has been largely eliminated. Industrial products such as steel and ships became leading export items, reflecting a successful reorientation of the economy toward heavy industries. With the advent of the 1960s, moreover, such consumer durables as automobiles, transistorized radios, TV sets, tape recorders and other electric and electronic products began to appear, penetrating Western markets.

This structural change in exports is indicated in Table 3.2. Cotton textiles, which were the major Japanese export, accounting for nearly 25 percent of the total exports in 1950, disappeared from the list of the top 10 export items in 1970—so did other types of textiles such as silk and rayon fabrics, which were replaced by modern synthetic fabrics. This concomitant occurrence—a decline of traditional exports and a rise of high-technology exports with a greater emphasis on product differentiation—depicts a shifting pattern of the product-life cycles of exports, a pattern actively capitalized upon by Japanese manufacturers in their adaptation to a changing world. Here, Japan's strong ability to adapt to shifting demand and supply conditions in the world economy is clearly demonstrated.

In this connection, a study made by the Japanese government sheds light on the sources of Japan's export competitiveness relative to other industrial countries. As shown in Table 3.3, the growth of exports is attributed to four factors: scale, price, nonprice, and the growth of world trade. Japan's exports expanded at the average annual rate of 13.7 percent during the period of 1955-1963—the second highest next to that of Italy—and

Table 3.2. Japan's Top 10 Exports

1950	1955	1960	1965	1970
Cotton textiles (24.9)	Steel (12.9)	Steel (9.6)	Steel (15.3)	Steel (14.7)
Steel (8.7)	Cotton textiles (11.4)	Cotton textiles (8.7)	Ships (8.8)	Ships (7.3)
Rayon fabric (4.6)	Apparel (5.3)	Ships (7.1)	Cotton textiles (3.6)	Automobiles (6.9)
Copper (4.3)	Staple fabrics (4.1)	Apparel (5.4)	Apparel (3.4)	Transistor radios (3.6)
Ships (3.2)	Ships (3.9)	Transistor radios (3.6)	Automobiles (2.8)	Synthetic fiber & fabric (3.2)
Apparel (2.8)	Marine products (3.8)	Staple fabrics (2.9)	Marine products (2.7)	Optical instruments (2.6)
Silk fabric (2.7)	Rayon fabrics (3.0)	Toys (2.2)	Transistor radios (2.6)	Apparel (2.4)
Toys (1.4)	Toys (2.1)	Automobiles (1.9)	Synthetic fiber & fabric (2.2)	Tape recorders (2.3)
Staple fabrics (1.3)	Ceramics (2.1)	Footwear (1.8)	Optical instruments (2.1)	Plastics (2.2)
Textile machinery (1.2)	Chemical fertilizer (2.1)	Ceramics (1.7)	Toys (1.2)	TV sets (2.0)
The total share of top 10 exports (55.2)	(50.7)	(44.8)	(44.6)	(47.2)

Source: Japanese Ministry of International Trade and Industry, 1971–Tsushoh Hakusho [1971–White Paper on International Trade] (Tokyo: MITI, 1971).

Note: The figures in parentheses indicate the share of each export item in the total value of Japanese exports.

Table 3.3. Growth Factors of Exports Among 10 Industrial Countries

Country	1955–1963					1963–1970				
	Average annual growth rate of export	Scale factor	Price factor	Nonprice factor	Growth of world-trade	Average annual growth rate of export	Scale factor	Price factor	Nonprice factor	Growth of world-trade
Japan	13.7	5.0	1.2	2.0	5.5	18.2	5.8	0.9	3.1	8.4
Canada	3.9	2.1	0.6	-3.4	4.6	11.3	2.7	-2.0	3.0	7.6
U.S.	3.7	1.6	-1.6	-1.0	4.7	6.5	2.1	-1.6	-1.3	7.3
Benelux	7.5	1.9	1.0	-0.3	4.9	11.3	2.5	0.2	1.0	7.6
W. Germany	10.0	3.4	-1.9	3.5	5.0	10.8	2.5	0.0	0.7	7.6
France	6.6	2.9	0.8	-2.0	4.9	10.2	3.1	0.4	-0.8	7.5
Italy	14.9	3.2	3.0	3.1	5.6	13.1	2.8	0.9	1.5	7.9
U.K.	2.8	1.5	-2.4	-1.0	4.7	5.5	1.4	0.5	-3.6	7.2
Sweden	7.5	2.2	-0.4	0.8	4.9	8.8	2.4	-0.9	-0.1	7.4
Denmark	7.2	4.4	0.3	-2.3	4.8	7.3	2.5	0.9	-3.4	7.3

Source: Japanese Ministry of International Trade and Industry, 1972–Tsushoh Hakusho [1972–White Paper on International Trade] (Tokyo: MITI, 1972).

18.2 percent during the period of 1963–1970, exhibiting the highest rate among the 10 industrial countries compared.

Japan's ability to adapt to changing world conditions is reflected in high percentages of the growth-of-world-trade factor for both periods; 5.5 percent during the 1955–1963 period and 8.4 percent during the 1963–1970 period, contributing most to Japan's export growth in each period.

Also significant is the relatively large size of scale factor. Here, scale economies are perhaps the most important element, leading to rapid productivity gains and cost reductions. As can be expected from such productivity gains, price was another important factor in Japan's export expansion, particularly during the 1955–1963 period. Yet nonprice factors contributed more to export growth than price factors in both periods, especially during the 1963–1970 period. Nonprice factors include supply and delivery capacities, quality, variety, advertising, service, and other marketing and promotional activities. The increased importance of nonprice factors, notably in the second period, is consistent with the shift of Japan's exports toward more sophisticated and differentiated products, such as automobiles, TV sets, and other consumer durables, as we have seen in Table 3.2.

The scale, price, and nonprice factors, although separately identified and treated as such, are closely interrelated. The scale factor, for example, has enhanced such a nonprice factor as the readiness of supplies. Cost reductions achieved through the productivity gain have enabled Japanese manufacturers not only to maintain price competitiveness but also to allocate even greater expenditures for marketing and promotional efforts. The scale factor thus strongly reinforced other competitive elements.

A question now arises as to how Japan alone was able to attain such a comparatively large scale. The quickly expanded scale of operation in Japanese industry was closely related to a high rate of capital accumulation— a buildup of productive capacity in new modern industries. This buildup was in large measure accomplished by the acquisition of Western technology and by financial and administrative assistance rendered by the government. In fact, the Japanese readily acknowledge the contribution of imported technology to the improvement of their industrial structure:

. . . it cannot be denied that, as the outcome of the technology acquired from overseas, there has been notable achievement in many fields of industry in connection with modernization of equipment, improvement of the quality of products, development of new products, and reduction of costs. Access to advanced technology has had no small effect upon the postwar change of Japan's industrial structure, and has been the key factor in bringing about the so-called technological transformation.[7]

Of course, Japanese manufacturers did not simply imitate Western industrial arts. As discussed in Chapter 5, they modified, improved, and perfected many imported technologies through adaptive R & D efforts. Moreover, in the 1960s the Japanese began to produce their own original technology. By and large, imported technology must have contributed to the modernization of Japanese industry more significantly in the 1950s than in the 1960s, since its technological dependence on the West was much greater in the former period. Besides, as noted in Chapter 2, with the relaxation of government controls in 1961, moving from the positive to the negative approval standard, comparatively less significant technology, including that simply representing brand names, also began to be imported in large numbers. Such technologies were attracted by Japan's expanding markets and did not directly improve its industrial capacity.

Capital Formation
The rapid orientation of the Japanese economy toward heavy and chemical industries in the postwar period entailed waves of new capital investment which provided the basis for Japan's miracle growth. For example, during the 1950s gross domestic capital formation ranged from 23.5 percent to 38.2 percent of GNP. In this section we examine the effects of technology imports on capital formation during the 1950s. My focus on this period is due partly to my basic supposition that it was mainly during the 1950s that imported technology played a truly significant role in modernizing Japan's industrial capacity—and due more importantly to the availability of statistics for my analysis.

In 1961 MITI conducted a comprehensive survey on various aspects of foreign technology absorption during the period of 1950–1961. As is with any survey findings based upon questionnaire methods, the information collected by MITI is not as complete as would be desirable. But the MITI survey provides us with enough interesting information for our purposes (see Notes on the MITI License Survey in Appendix).

Let us first take a look at the overall relationship between technology imports (category A) and the amount of investment in producer's equipment over the period of 1950–1960 (Table 3.4). Note that in those years in which the volume of technology imports was large, investment in producer's equipment was similarly high. Their coincident movements become clearer when the ratio of investment in producer's equipment to GNP is compared with the trend of technology imports; ups and downs in both variables are closely associated with each other except for the period of 1956–1957.

A more direct link between technology imports and investment is revealed by the MITI survey. The extent to which imported technologies stimulated investments in the manufacturing sector is shown in Table 3.5. Looking at the period of 1950–1960 as a whole, we can make several interesting observations.

First, imported technologies were <u>directly</u> responsible for 27.7 percent of the total investments in equipment made by technology-importing manufacturing firms, although year-to-year variations existed. Second, imported-technology-based investments accounted for about 9 percent of the total value of investments in equipment, buildings, and other productive facilities made by the entire manufacturing sector. This percentage, however, understates the true magnitude since the A-numbers indicate the values of investment in equipment and, moreover, they are based on a sample survey that represented 77 percent of technology-importing manufacturing firms; yet the C-numbers represent the entire manufacturing industry and include the values of investment, not only in equipment but also in buildings and other productive facilities. Third, 32.7 percent of the entire manufacturing sector's investment facilities is accounted for by those equipment investments made by technology-importing firms. Again, the true magnitude is understated for the same reasons cited above. All this seems to suggest that imported technologies did play a significant role in stimulating a high level of capital investment during the 1950s.

Table 3.4. Technology Imports, Investment in Producer's Equipment, and GNP: 1950–1960 (in billions of yen)

Year	(A) The number of technology imports[a]	(B) Investment in producer's equipment	(C) GNP	(D) B/C	(E) Increase or decrease in D	(F) Increase or decrease in A
1950	27	389.9	3,946.7	9.8		
1951	101	609.3	5,444.2	11.2	+	+
1952	142	712.6	6,118.0	11.7	+	+
1953	102	800.7	7,084.8	11.3	−	−
1954	82	762.2	7,461.8	10.2	−	−
1955	71	778.8	8,229.8	9.5	−	−
1956	143	1,374.9	9,287.8	14.8	+	+
1957	118	1,693.2	10,149.8	16.7	+	−
1958	90	1,649.6	10,394.7	15.9	−	−
1959	153	2,170.2	12,572.5	17.3	+	+
1960	327	3,069.5	14,664.9	20.9	+	+

Sources: Technology imports from 1970–Gaikoku Gijutsu Dohnyu Nenji Hohkoku [1970–Annual Report on Absorption of Foreign Technology] [Tokyo: Printing Office, The Ministry of Finance, 1972]; and gross national product and investment in producer's equipment from Economic Planning Agency, Japanese government, Japanese Economic Statistics (Tokyo: Printing Office, The Ministry of Finance, 1961).

[a]Category A

Table 3.5. Technology Imports and Investments in Producers' Durable Equipment in Manufacturing Industries, 1950–1960 (in millions of yen)

Year	A	B	C	A/B	A/C	B/C
1950	595	2,064	95,800	28.8	0.6	2.2
1951	5,878	25,958	314,700	22.6	1.9	8.5
1952	10,606	37,520	245,500	28.3	4.3	15.3
1953	19,415	73,513	243,900	26.4	8.0	30.1
1954	15,042	56,585	268,200	26.6	5.6	21.1
1955	17,815	75,408	245,800	23.6	7.2	30.7
1956	34,819	127,283	459,300	27.4	7.6	27.7
1957	71,867	249,836	716,400	28.8	10.0	34.9
1958	92,099	268,643	594,000	34.3	15.5	45.2
1959	96,901	324,920	766,500	29.8	12.6	42.4
1960	113,193	487,756	1,345,300	23.2	8.4	36.3
Total	478,230	1,729,486	5,295,400	27.7	9.0	32.7

Source: Japanese Ministry of International Trade and Industry, Gaikoku Gijutsu Dohnyu no Genjoh to Mondaiten [Current Status and Problems of Foreign Technology Absorption] (Tokyo: MITI; 1962).

A—Amount of investment in equipment directly related to imported technology made by technology-importing firms

B—Total amount of investment in equipment made by technology-importing firms in manufacturing industries

C—Total amount of investment in equipment, buildings, and other productive facilities made by manufacturing industries

As seen earlier, the development of heavy and chemical industries was given top priority, and efforts were initially made to channel advanced foreign technologies mainly into these industries. It can therefore be expected that a correspondingly large amount of new investment was directly induced by imported technologies in these industries. The impact of imported technologies on investments in six major manufacturing industries is shown in Table 3.6. It is noteworthy that as much as 41.6 percent of the chemical industry's investment in equipment was directly stimulated by imported technologies. Electrical machinery is another industry whose productive capacity was enhanced by technological borrowing; 25.8 percent of its investment in equipment was based on imported technologies. Predictably enough, the corresponding ratio was small for the textile industry that had already been a well established industry.

Aside from those investments necessitated by imported technology, many other types of investments also must have been indirectly induced both

inside and outside the technology-importing firms. Since imported technologies were mostly of more advanced and drastically different nature,
their introduction often required greater technical adjustments in productive facilities. When the technology-importing firm's capacity was expanded, its suppliers and subcontractors also had to make necessary
production adjustments. All this led to rising demands for new machinery
and equipment, which in turn expanded the capital goods sector. This type
of interfirm and interindustry investment linkages were the vital mechanism for starting a chain of investment activities throughout the economy.
The snowballing effect was further intensified by the unique web of industrial connections spun within each keiretsu group—the postwar version of
the old zaibatsu—composed of a large number of closely affiliated firms,
subsidiaries, and subcontractors.[8] No doubt, a fierce rivalry among the
groups for their market domination added fuel to the engine of industrial
expansion.

The magnitude of all this multiplied effect of investment is evident in the
results of time-series regression analysis shown in Table 3.7. Part A shows
the relation between the value of imported-technology-based investments
in equipment (independent variable) and the total value of investment in
equipment made by technology-importing firms (dependent variable),

Table 3.6. Technology Imports and Investments in Equipment by Selected Industry,
1950–1960 (in millions of yen)

	A	B	C	A/B	A/C	B/C
Manufacturing industry	478,230	1,729,486	5,295,400	27.7	9.0	32.7
Electrical machinery	44,286	171,445	439,500	25.8	10.1	39.0
Nonelectrical machinery	5,754	38,601	183,000	14.9	3.1	21.1
Chemicals	207,413	498,678	873,500	41.6	21.3	57.1
Iron and steel	85,947	523,793	1,064,800	16.4	0.7	49.2
Transport equipment	23,455	143,543	391,200	16.3	6.1	36.7
Textiles	706	13,091	319,300	5.4	0.2	41.0

Source: Japanese Ministry of International Trade and Industry, Gaikoku Gijutsu
Dohnyu no Genjoh to Mondaiten [Current Status and Problems of Foreign
Absorption] (Tokyo: MITI, 1962).

A—Amount of investment in equipment directly related to imported technology
made by technology-importing firms

B—Total amount of investment in equipment made by technology-importing firms

C—Total amount of investment in equipment, buildings, and other productive
facilities made by each entire industry

Table 3.7. Significance of Induced Investment (Linear Regression Analysis)

Industry	Coefficient of regression	Coefficient of determination
A. relation between (1) the value of imported-technology-based investment in equipment and (2) the total value of investment in equipment made by technology-importing firms		
Manufacturing Industry (1950–1960)	26.2	0.91[a]
Electrical machinery (1951–1960)	2.8	0.94[a]
Nonelectrical machinery (1951–1960)	7.2	0.83[a]
Chemicals (1951–1960)	1.2	0.84[a]
Iron and steel (1951–1960)	3.9	0.50[b]
Transport equipment (1951–1960)	5.3	0.83[a]
Textiles (1952–1960)	5.2	0.11
B. relation between (1) the value of imported-technology-based investment in equipment and (2) the total value of investment by all firms		
Manufacturing Industry (1950–1960)	6.4	0.56[a]
Electrical machinery (1951–1960)	7.3	0.71[a,c]
Nonelectrical machinery (1951–1960)	31.4	0.82[a]
Chemicals (1951–1960)	2.5	0.72[a]
Iron and steel (1951–1960)	8.0	0.45[b]
Transport equipment (1953–1960)	−0.2	0.04
Textiles (1952–1960)	0.02	0.02

Sources: Data used for the above analysis came from Japanese Ministry of International Trade and Industry, Gaikoku Gijutsu Dohnyu no Genjoh to Mondaiten [Current Status and Problems of Foreign Technology Absorption] (Tokyo: MITI, 1962); and Hohjin Kigyo Tokei [Statistics on Corporation] (Tokyo: The Ministry of Finance, 1962).

[a]Statistically significant at the 0.01 level

[b]Statistically significant at the 0.05 level

[c]Significantly autocorrelated at the 0.01 level

while Part B relates the former (independent variable) to each industry's total value of investments in equipment, buildings and other productive facilities (dependent variable).

Three observations are in order. First, the correlations revealed in Part A are, without exception, higher in all industries than those revealed in Part B. This is, of course, exactly what should be expected from the different natures of the dependent variables; the first set uses the total value of investment in equipment by technology-importing firms alone, whereas the second set uses the total value of investments not only in equipment but also in buildings and other productive facilities made by all the firms in each industry. Secondly, those industries that acquired much foreign technology, that is, electrical machinery, nonelectrical machinery, and chemicals, show higher degrees of correlation in both sets of analyses than other industries. The coefficients of determination for the former industries are 0.94, 0.83, and 0.84, respectively, in the first set—and 0.71, 0.82, and 0.72, respectively, in the second set. Again, this pattern is consistent; the investment-inducing effect of foreign technology, if any, should naturally be stronger in those industries which absorbed larger amounts of imported technology. Thirdly, it should be noted that those firms which actively imported foreign technologies were mostly large firms, and that they were therefore financially capable of responding to investment opportunities—a factor that facilitated induced investments.

All in all, there is no doubt that the government-controlled acquisition of foreign technologies played a significant role in creating investment opportunities. Indeed, this unique experience of Japan's capacity building is officially recognized in the following observation made by the government in 1962:

Generally speaking, equipment investments in connection with technological innovation have been increasingly poured in during the past ten years. . . . There are various factors which have caused an increase in equipment investments recently. Although it is natural that competition is intense under a free enterprise system, efforts toward bringing up the level of technology to that of advanced countries is one factor which has created competition in the induction of foreign technology, which, in turn, has resulted in excessive investment competition. Also by expanding their production capacity, the various enterprises are engaging in a fierce competition to secure as large a share of the market as possible without considering their margin of profit . . . investments for investment goods industries had increased greatly and as a result, the demand and supply balance of related industries had tended to become tight, which, in turn, resulted in more investments. This is the so-called effect of "investments, creating more investments."[9]

The word "induction" in this quotation refers to the government-controlled acquisition of foreign industrial arts.

All this suggests that the high rate of capital formation provided the link between Japan's acquisition of foreign technology and its export performance, and that so far as the 1950s are concerned, Japanese export expansion was concomitant to the development of new productive capacity under the main stimulus of technological borrowing, accompanied by a rapid reduction of production costs.

Import Substitution
An array of import tariffs and quotas were imposed by the government both as a short-term policy to optimize the allocation of scarce foreign exchange and as a long-term policy to develop domestic industries through import substitution. Because of government restrictions on foreign direct investments in Japanese industries, coupled with generally cautious attitudes taken by Western manufacturers toward direct investments in Japan in the early 1950s, licensing agreements were the predominant form of technology imports. Thus licensing served as a substitute for exports for the Western manufacturers while it assisted Japanese industries to develop new productive capacities with minimum foreign controls of enterprises.

To measure the extent to which domestic output under licenses replaced imports, let us assume that without imported technologies, imports equivalent in value to "licensed-manufactures sold in domestic markets" would have been made. We will then regard the sum of the value of licensed-manufactures sold in home markets and the value of actual imports as the total value of "imports." Again we will be concerned solely with the period of 1950–1960 for the reasons stated in the preceding section.

Table 3.8 shows the ratios of the value of licensed-manufactures sold in home markets to the total value of "imports" for six major manufacturing industries over the period of 1950–1960. This import-substitution ratio was over 90 percent for electrical machinery from the start; this may partly reflect the fact that in the prewar days this industry used to have many technical tie-ups with foreign firms, which were quickly restored immediately upon the enactment of the Foreign Investment Law. The development of the electrical machinery industry was also encouraged from the beginning under the import substitution policy. Moreover, this industry had a relatively good industrial base, which made it immediately possible to manufacture under foreign licenses.

The ratios for the other five industries were less than 50 percent at the beginning, but they rapidly increased throughout the period; the ratio rose

Table 3.8. Import Substitution through Licensing, 1950–1960. The Ratio of Licensed-Manufactures Sold in Domestic Markets to the Total Value of Imports (in percentage)

Industry	1950	1951	1952	1953	1954	1955	1956	1957	1958	1959	1960	Average
Electrical machinery	90.4	94.9	95.9	89.6	90.9	92.6	93.7	95.8	96.2	96.6	97.5	94.0
Nonelectrical machinery	22.8	44.1	39.6	32.8	30.3	38.5	46.1	40.2	41.0	45.6	52.6	39.4
Chemicals	n.a.	13.8	24.7	31.5	34.7	39.9	44.5	49.3	58.9	62.9	68.8	42.9
Iron and steel	n.a.	48.5	66.5	82.7	87.9	92.2	94.1	45.2	93.3	92.1	90.6	81.1
Transport equipment	n.a.	1.0	2.3	8.0	33.3	52.1	59.8	61.5	69.0	63.8	56.5	40.7
Textiles	n.a.	n.a.	14.4	22.1	50.6	51.3	52.9	50.5	61.3	65.1	65.8	53.5

Source: Japanese Ministry of International Trade and Industry, Gaikoku Gijutsu Dohnyu no Genjoh to Mondaiten [Current Status and Problems of Foreign Technology Absorption] (Tokyo: MITI, 1962).

n.a.—not available

from 23 percent to 53 percent in nonelectrical machinery; from 14 percent to 69 percent in chemicals; from 49 percent to as much as 91 percent for iron and steel; from a miniscule 1 percent to 57 percent in transport equipment; and from 14 percent to 66 percent in textiles. Thus the import substitution effect was substantial in all six industries.

It should be noted, however, that the total value of "imports" used above includes those import demands which came into existence only as a result of Japan's industrial expansion achieved by technological assimilation. In other words, the process of import substitution in this particular case was of a dynamic nature in the sense that those licensed-manufactures not only satisfied existing demand for imports—that is, import substitution in a static sense—but also expanded national income through a familiar multiplier effect, leading to more import demands, which were, in turn, simultaneously satisfied by the licensed-manufactures at home. Furthermore, in many cases imported technologies had to be developed for commercial uses. Included in the value of "imports" were, therefore, also those demands which would have never existed had it not been for adaptive research efforts made on the part of the Japanese.

Domestic Markets versus Exports
It is often observed that Japan's postwar industrial expansion has been more strongly oriented to domestic than to foreign markets. Usually marshalled as evidence for this view is a relatively small ratio of Japan's export (or imports) to GNP.[10] Leon Hollerman, for example, observes: "Despite the fact that the quantity of exports practically quadrupled during the decade prior to 1971, Japanese industry in the postwar period became less, rather than more, export oriented."[11] He points out that the ratio of exports to the national income were 12.8 percent in 1960 compared with 23.1 percent in 1936.[12] Similar observations have been made by many other economists.[13]

Indeed, the assertion that the domestic market, rather than exports, was the primary basis for economic growth sounds quite "paradoxical" for a small island economy which depends so much on overseas markets for industrial resources and whose export drive is so famed. In this regard, our analysis of the import substitution effect of licensed manufactures seems to shed considerable light on this paradox.

As seen above, the development of heavy and chemical industries was fostered under foreign licenses. Since these capital-intensive sectors were extensive in linkage effects, a series of induced domestic capital investments were triggered in the related industries. This high rate of capital formation supported a phenomenal economic growth which in turn created huge internal demands for those products manufactured under licenses—the effect we have identified as the dynamic case of import substitution. Yet, as intended by the Foreign Investment Law, the acquisition of foreign technologies itself was, at the same time, aimed at strengthening Japan's exports.

Again, drawing upon the MITI license survey, let us look at the sales distribution of licensed manufactures between domestic and export markets (Table 3.9), and the proportion of the sales of licensed manufactures in each industry's total exports (Table 3.10). With the exception of the textile industry, the domestic market absorbed 80 to 90 percent of each industry's licensed output during the period of 1950–1960.

Yet, the ratio of the exports of licensed manufactures to each industry's total exports was considerably significant. These ratios for electrical machinery, nonelectrical machinery, chemicals, and iron and steel, for example, steadily climbed to the range of 25 to 50 percent toward the end of the 1950s. Thus the exports of those products manufactured with imported technology, though initially insignificant, swiftly increased and came to account for a sizable proportion of each industry's total exports.

Indeed, as much as 50 percent of Japan's exports of electrical machinery in 1960 involved those products manufactured under licenses. Chemicals and iron and steel also exhibited similarly high percentages of such exports. Although the corresponding ratio for transport equipment was small, it should be noted that a large part of this industry's inputs, such as steel and machinery for ships and automobiles, came from other industries which were producing under licenses. In fact, if we take into account all the input-output relationships among industries, the contribution of

Table 3.9. Sales Distribution of Licensed-Manufactures between Export and Domestic Markets, 1950–1960 (in percentage)

Industry		1950	1951	1952	1953	1954	1955	1956	1957	1958	1959	1960
Electrical	A	93.1	91.3	98.1	97.6	97.6	98.2	98.3	96.2	95.2	92.3	89.9
machinery	B	6.9	8.7	1.9	2.4	2.4	1.8	1.7	3.8	4.8	7.7	10.1
Nonelectrical	A	—	98.5	99.2	96.4	96.3	90.8	91.7	90.9	90.7	93.7	94.3
machinery	B	—	1.5	0.8	3.6	3.7	9.2	8.3	9.1	9.3	6.3	5.7
Chemicals	A	—	99.1	98.9	95.9	90.5	82.1	82.9	83.0	82.0	80.7	85.8
	B	—	0.9	1.1	4.1	9.5	17.9	17.1	17.0	18.0	19.3	14.2
Iron and steel	A	—	94.9	95.7	92.3	82.7	85.4	89.5	84.5	85.4	84.8	86.0
	B	—	5.1	4.3	7.7	17.3	14.6	10.5	15.5	14.6	15.2	14.0
Transport	A	—	82.4	94.7	98.6	99.7	94.7	96.4	97.8	95.8	97.1	94.6
equipment	B	—	7.6	5.3	1.4	0.3	5.3	3.6	2.2	4.2	2.9	5.4
Textiles	A	—	—	33.4	34.1	40.7	31.3	42.2	43.4	40.9	42.2	43.4
	B	—	—	66.6	65.9	59.3	68.7	57.8	56.6	59.1	57.8	56.6

Source: Japanese Ministry of International Trade and Industry, Gaikoku Gijutsu Dohnyu no Genjoh to Mondaiten [Current Status and Problems of Foreign Technology Absorption] (Tokyo: MITI, 1962).

A—Domestic market
B—Export market

Table 3.10. Sales of Licensed-Manufactures in Total Value of Exports by Industry, 1950–1960 (in percentage)

Industry	1950	1951	1952	1953	1954	1955	1956	1957	1958	1959	1960
Electrical machinery	6.8	11.7	6.3	31.2	24.4	28.2	17.3	29.1	44.5	43.8	50.2
Nonelectrical machinery	—	0.3	0.9	4.9	1.9	6.2	7.6	11.9	14.8	9.1	8.8
Chemicals	—	0.05	0.2	1.3	2.8	7.6	8.6	10.2	15.7	25.2	24.3
Iron and steel	—	0.2	0.3	3.8	10.3	7.9	10.7	22.0	22.9	39.0	35.6
Transport equipment	—	0.1	0.2	0.1	0.1	1.2	0.6	0.4	1.0	0.7	1.5
Textiles	—	—	1.1	3.1	2.7	4.8	4.0	4.8	6.0	6.1	6.0

Source: Japanese Ministry of International Trade and Industry, Gaikoku Gijutsu Dohnyu no Genjoh to Mondaiten [Current Status and Problems of Foreign Technology Absorption] (Tokyo: MITI, 1962).

licensed manufactures to Japan's export performance would be much greater than implied by the ratios shown in the table.[14]

The corresponding ratio for textiles was, nevertheless, extremely small. Foreign technologies acquired by this industry were mostly related to the production of new synthetic fibers, but Japan's export of such products remained relatively small during the 1950s since cotton textiles were still the industry's major export item.

There were undoubtedly important interactions between import substitution and export expansion. The swift expansion of the domestic market under the stimulus of import substitution enabled Japanese manufacturers to attain a sufficiently high level of output for scale economies and to install the latest possible machinery and equipment. Assembly-type operations were quickly adopted and a variety of automated production processes were introduced. All these activities led to a substantial rise in productivity and trade competitiveness.

On the other hand, export markets provided strong incentives for upgrading the quality and variety of Japanese products. As we saw earlier, technological absorption was designed to modernize the export structure. Indeed, it is not unreasonable to argue that without Japan's export drive in advanced Western countries, the quality and variety of Japan's industrial output would never have been so quickly advanced, and the modernization process of the industrial structure with emphasis on heavy and chemical industries would have been considerably retarded.

In short, export markets provided a major stimulus for the qualitative improvements of Japan's industrial structure and output, whereas the growing domestic market contributed more to the quantitative aspect of output, that is, a realization of scale economies.[15]

Placed in perspective, the phenomenal expansions of both domestic and export markets were concurrent and mutually reinforcing—and were underlined by the same basic force, technological assimilation. Depending upon the focus of analysis, one may be tempted to emphasize either the domestic or export market as the basis of Japan's postwar economic

growth. But it is futile to try to make a clear-cut judgment as to which
market was the cause for the economic growth, since, as we have seen
above, the two markets grew as the composite whole of Japan's postwar
industrialization and technological transformation.

It should be noted in passing that Japan's economic structure thus built
upon its successful import substitution in manufacturing industries has
come to make its import structure less dependent on foreign manufactures
but more dependent on foreign industrial raw materials and foodstuffs; in
1971, for example, the import of manufactures accounted for only 27.9
percent of the total imports.[16]

4 Internationalization of the Domestic Market

A Rise of Foreign Business Operations in Japan

Throughout the fifties, due to a weak balance of payments position—and perhaps more importantly, due to the fear of foreign invasion of domestic industries—the government carefully screened each technology purchase proposal and approved only those which had some reasonable promise of achieving the goals set by the Foreign Investment Law. As we saw in earlier chapters, the acquisition of foreign technology, an instrument for Japan's design of industrialization, played a vital role in cementing the foundation of Japan's postwar economic development.

Since in the early 1950s the Japanese economy was still prostrate from the damage of war, there was little interest on the part of Western manufacturers to invest in Japan. To be sure, some international corporations, notably in the petroleum and petrochemical fields, made inroads in the Japanese markets as a part of their global operations—but these were still an exception. Consequently, it was mostly the Japanese who took the initiative to acquire technology, and most Western firms were quite willing to supply it under licensing agreements. Viewed with the vantage of hindsight, there was less danger of foreign take-over of domestic industries than some government officials and business leaders had feared.

The vigorous expansion of the economy that became especially evident with the advent of the sixties, however, did begin to attract the interest of many foreign manufacturers, particularly American firms, to invest in Japan's growing domestic markets. This development is reflected in the trend of technology purchase contracts and the inflow of direct foreign investment during the period of 1950–1971, as shown in Table 4.1.

Government Intervention

Aside from the question of whether or not its fear of foreign capital domination was truly justified, the government's tight control of technology imports on the whole was, as might have been expected, quite beneficial to Japanese industry, since Japan's dire need of advanced foreign technologies put it in a weak bargaining position vis-à-vis foreign suppliers. Government controls were exercised not only to channel foreign technologies into specific key industrial sectors—as seen earlier in the official lists of desired industrial know-how, but also to insure favorable contract terms

Table 4.1. Technology Imports and Foreign Investment in Subsidiaries and Joint Ventures in Japan, 1950–1970

Year	Number of technology contracts approved (category A)	Foreign investment in subsidiaries and joint ventures (in $1,000)
1950	27	2,572
1951	101	11,646
1952	142	7,166
1953	102	2,687
1954	82	2,467
1955	71	2,309
1956	143	5,360
1957	118	7,282
1958	90	3,698
1959	153	14,561
1960	327	31,593
1961	320	40,170
1962	328	22,618
1963	564	42,656
1964	500	30,645
1965	472	44,643
1966	601	39,812
1967	638	32,051
1968	1,061	67,141
1969	1,154	70,432
1970	1,330	114,486
1971	1,546	255,463

Sources: Technology imports from Japanese Science and Technology Agency, 1971–Gaikoku Gijutsu Dohnyu Nenji Hohkoku [1971–Annual Report on Absorption of Foreign Technology] (Tokyo: Printing Office, The Ministry of Finance, 1972); and foreign investment from the Bank of Japan, Economic Statistics Annual (Tokyo: the Bank of Japan, 1967 and 1972).

and to improve the bargaining position of Japanese firms. For this interference the government was criticized in an OECD report:

Apart from the application of general principles of "exceptional adjustment", it happens that, after the Japanese and the foreign partner have agreed on the terms of a contract, the authorities make approval conditional on amendments, usually in favor of the former. The scope of the technology is frequently changed; the royalties and initial payments are reduced; minimum royalties and back royalties are eliminated; arrangements must be made for the Japanese partner to get privileged access to certain foreign markets; provisions are disallowed under which the Japanese partner renounces manufacture after the expiry of the contract or to make certain competitive products; sub-licensing is made subject to further governmental approval; undertakings are deleted under which the Japanese partner would hand over a list of his customers at the end of the contract;

the duration of the contract is reduced; automatic renewal is excluded, etc. All these changes of the terms of his contract are imposed upon the resident (as well as the non-resident) whether he wishes it or not, although, as long as they are in favour, he would be unlikely to object to this form of official guardianship over his interests. Government action is generally supposed to be for the good of its nationals, but in this case it takes an unusual direct form of interference with bona fide private contracts.[1]

The behavior of the Japanese government in intervening between Japanese buyers of technology and the Western suppliers may be better understood in terms of Stephen Hymer's theory of international operation.[2] He explains the movement of direct investment capital as a consequence of the investing firm's desire to expand or prolong its unique advantage—a theory referred to in Chapter 1. Discussing the choice confronting the possessor of a certain technical advantage—whether to enter a foreign market by licensing or direct investment—Hymer reasons that when the foreign market is imperfect (that is, when only a few firms exist), a bilateral monopoly problem makes cooperation through licensing difficult. On the other hand, when the foreign market is highly competitive (that is, when many potential buyers of technology exist) licensing is almost certain, since the market mechanism fully appropriates the return to the seller. Hymer generalizes that it is the market imperfection, therefore, that leads the possessor of the technical advantage "to choose to supersede the market for his advantage."[3]

Applying Hymer's theory to the Japanese case, one may then ask: What type of market structure did the Japanese import market for technology exhibit during the fifties? There is abundant evidence that the economy was in a fluxionary state of development, and that therefore furious competition prevailed among Japanese firms in their efforts to acquire foreign technology as a means of securing a larger share in their domestic markets— a familiar manifestation of Japan's "excessive competition."[4]

According to Hymer's theory, the Japanese market was at that time more favorable to licensing operations than to direct investment. The foreign possessor of technical advantage did not need "to supersede the market" because the highly competitive market would allow it to extract full monopolistic returns to its advantage. From the Japanese government's point of view, however, this would have meant that the competitive market was in danger of succumbing to foreign monopolistic exploitation. Consequently, the government found it necessary to intervene in the market by exercising what may be considered "countervailing power" to the monopolistic possessors of technology through the intricate regulatory mechanism it set up under the Foreign Investment Law.

But that intervention in turn raises a series of questions: If government intervention made the market less perfect for would-be licensors by curbing its competitive tendencies, did they then become interested in direct investment to exploit their technological advantages by themselves? In fact this alternative was more strictly controlled by the Japanese government than licensing. Then were they discouraged from supplying technologies as a result? The fact is that Western firms continued to provide technologies to the Japanese under licensing agreements despite government interventions. Why were they so willing?

Although severely criticized by OECD, government intervention, after all, probably did not matter much to most suppliers of technology during the 1950s. In the first place, Japanese licensees paid large royalties as they exploited imported technology and expanded their market shares both at home and abroad—with startling success, as we saw in Chapter 3. Even if the per unit royalty rate—a contract provision closely watched by the government—was kept relatively low, the large volumes of output assured satisfactory returns to the licensors. In fact, license fees quickly became a heavy "burden" on the invisible trade account of Japan's balance of payments.[5]

Moreover, the technologies initially supplied were in most cases relatively mature and conventional by Western, and particularly U.S., standards. The large technology gap between Japan and the United States which existed in the 1950s appeared to grow even wider at that time because of the high level of R & D activities in the United States—and this made U.S. firms relatively magnanimous about supplying technology by licenses.

During the 1950s Western manufacturers were generally unfamiliar with the sociocultural environment for doing business in Japan—a problem still existing to the present, though perhaps to a lesser degree—this probably helped induce them to use licensing operations to feel out the Japanese market.

The 1960s witnessed a vigorous expansion of the Japanese economy; it was then that Western suppliers of technology began to feel the pressure of government interference in both licensing operations and direct foreign investment. By then, the interest of Western manufacturers in investment in Japanese industry had grown appreciably, since Japan demonstrated a high rate of economic growth at home and of export expansion in world markets. What is more, since the Japanese purchased more of the latest and most sophisticated types of industrial know-how, Western manufacturers, notably American ones, became reluctant to sell technologies simply through licensing.

Further, as earlier licensing agreements with the Japanese neared expiration in the 1960s, Western manufacturers were threatened with loss of royalty income and confronted with "serious problems for their future efforts to capitalize on Japan's profit opportunities."[6] Under these circumstances they naturally became more interested in acquiring ownership interests in exchange for supplying technology in order to secure a longer-term share of the profits. In other words, they resorted to what may be called a technology-cum-investment strategy.

With this turn of events, greater conflicts inevitably developed between Western suppliers of technology and the Japanese government despite the latter's move to liberalize its controls over technology and capital imports and to reduce administrative delays in validating contracts; the market forces had by then clearly outgrown the restricted arena of operations, which was being widened only slowly by the Japanese government. Prior to the first round of the liberalization of capital controls implemented in July 1967, wholly-foreign-owned investments were almost totally restricted, with the exception of the so-called "yen-basis" investments.[7]

The growing interest of U.S. manufacturers in the technology-cum-investment strategy was, for example, indicated in the following statements made by several business executives in the late 1950s in response to a National Industrial Conference Board survey on foreign licensing:

Licensing is an effective way of developing manufacturing in highly competitive or newly developing markets, but when markets are developed, ownership of the operations should be the aim for better returns.

It is anticipated that there will be an increasing effort to receive compensation based on a fair share of manufacturing profits via dividends on capital stock, rather than on the basis of royalty income on units of production. This arrangement has the benefit of relating the payment to us with the actual benefit to the licensee, thereby protecting both ourselves and the licensee.

We feel that licensing is an effective and also profitable way of exploiting a foreign market. More recently, however, we have felt that a pure licensing arrangement is not as desirable as a licensing arrangement in conjunction with investment in the licensee on our part. We feel that the amount of royalty which we can reasonably expect the licensee to pay is not as much as we can earn in the form of return on investment.[8]

To accommodate the interests of both Western and local Japanese industries, joint ventures thus became the predominant form of direct foreign investments in Japan.

How effective Western firms' strategy of combining technology sales with direct investment has been is indicated by the findings of a 1967 survey made by MITI on foreign joint ventures in Japan. As much as 83 percent of the responding Japanese partners (270 out of a total of 327 Japanese companies) stated that acquisition of technology was a primary motive for accepting foreign capital. On the other hand, 79 percent of the responding foreign partners (326 of the 414 foreign partners surveyed) explained that the growing local markets were a major attraction for investing in Japan.[9]

Advance of Multinational Corporations
The Japanese government has been keeping close watch on the advance of foreign-based multinational corporations or what they define as "world enterprises" in terms of Fortune's list of large corporations. For example, MITI's survey of foreign-affiliated firms in 1972 provides a breakdown by industry on the advance of such enterprises (Table 4.2).

United States corporations are the largest group of investors operating in Japan, accounting for 84 percent of the total as of September 1971. Of the 200 largest U.S. corporations, 92 (46 percent) had already made an advance into Japanese industry, compared with only 17 of the 80 largest

Table 4.2. Advances of Foreign World Enterprises in Japan (as of June 30, 1971)

Industry	The number of the largest 200 U.S. corporations[a]	(The number of those with ownership interest greater than 20%)	The number of the largest 100 European corporations[a]	(The number of those with ownership interest greater than 20%
Food processing	36	(13)	9	(2)
Textiles	5	(1)	1	(–)
Paper and pulp	9	(3)	1	(–)
Chemicals	16	(10)	10	(6)
Pharmaceuticals	8	(7)	1	(–)
Petroleum	21	(11)	11	(1)
Rubber and tire	5	(4)	3	(1)
Stone, clay, and glass	3	(3)	1	(–)
Metals, ferrous and nonferrous	17	(5)	20	(3)
Metal products	11	(2)	1	(–)
Nonelectric machinery	19	(11)	5	(1)
Electric machinery	19	(10)	7	(2)
Transport equipment	23	(9)	9	(–)
Precision machinery	4	(2)	–	(–)
Others	4	(1)	1	(1)
Total	200	(92)	80	(17)

Source: Japanese Ministry of International Trade and Industry, Gaishikei Kigyo no Dohkoh [Trend of Foreign-Affiliated Enterprises] (Tokyo: Printing Office, The Ministry of Finance, 1972).

[a]Classified by Fortune magazine

European enterprises (21 percent). United States-based world enterprises are concentrated in such industries as food processing, petroleum, chemicals, nonelectrical machinery, electrical machinery, transport equipment, and pharmaceuticals, while chemicals and nonferrous metals are the two major areas in which European world enterprises moved.

In the face of its international commitment to accept more foreign investment, how will Japan, then, be able to cope with much deeper penetration by foreign interests? Japanese industries have already undergone a rapid reorganization through mergers and acquisitions to gain economies of scale and thereby to strengthen their competitive position. The Anti-Monopoly Law of 1947, enacted at the direction of the occupation authorities to break up economic concentrations of the zaibatsu groups, has been amended to permit the so-called "recession and rationalization cartels." These cartels were originally intended, as their nomenclature suggests, to assist those industries affected by the economic slowdowns in the 1950s and early 1960s. However, they came later to be utilized as a means to strengthen domestic industries against the liberalization of direct foreign investments in Japan. In 1966, for example, MITI asked the Fair Trade Commission, administrative organ of the Anti-Monopoly Law, to be tolerant to those mergers which were designed to increase domestic firms' competitiveness vis-à-vis foreign entrants.[10]

Indeed, those firms which had been previously broken up during the occupation years have gradually been combined. Notable examples were the mergers of Shin Mitsubishi Heavy Industries, Mitsubishi Nihon Heavy Industries, and Mitsubishi Shipbuilding and Engineering Industry, and of Yawata and Fuji Iron and Steel Co. The latter merger was particularly significant. When it was approved by the Fair Trade Commission in 1969, Yawata was the largest steel company in Japan and also the fourth largest in the world, while Fuji was the second in Japan as well as the fifth in the world.[11] Their mergers epitomized the leniency displayed by the Commission. Many other firms, although without any previous zaibatsu connections, similarly conglomerated into giant corporations. Consolidation movements were widespread not only in manufacturing but also in commerce and finance sectors. As a result, huge and powerful Japanese corporations emerged one after another. Fortune magazine listed four Japanese

corporations among the world's 100 largest in 1957; the number increased
to 14 in 1963 and to 21 in 1972.

It is important to note that the competitive strength of Japanese firms
should not be judged solely in terms of their individual size. There are
close associations among the firms comprising each keiretsu group—a
loosely affiliated industrial group which has emerged as an alternative
form of industrial constellation to the former zaibatsu groups, which were
controlled by their respective holding companies. Since the keiretsu group
embraces a number of heterogeneous, but mutually complementary, industries, it enjoys an extremely flexible form of conglomeration. The nucleus
of the groups is usually a bank or a general trading company. In fact, it
was the keiretsu banks that encouraged and directed mergers and acquisitions within each group throughout the postwar period.[12] Recently, however, the importance of the keiretsu banks has somewhat declined with
improved capital supply, and it is the general trading firms that now often
play the leadership role in charting new directions for their respective
groups. This trend is encouraged in part by increased overseas investment
activities of the keiretsu groups, activities which call for the assistance of
the trading companies' global intelligence networks and their proficiency
in international operations.

The Japanese government is also bent on encouraging the development of
indigenous technology to reduce the dependence of Japanese firms on
Western technologies. Tax credit is provided for R & D expenses and for
earnings from technology sales overseas. R & D expenditures in Japanese
industry increased at a much faster rate than in any other country in the
period of 1961–1970; they increased at an average annual rate of 20.6
percent in Japan, in contrast to 17.5 percent in France, 12.4 percent in
West Germany, 10.5 percent in the USSR, and 7.6 percent in the United
States.[13] Indeed, Japan's efforts to accelerate indigenous technological
progress are among the most positive side effects of capital liberalization.

The first official program of capital liberalization was initiated in June
1967, and completed after four rounds of decontrol, in August 1971. As
one might expect, this liberalization was closely synchronized with the
consolidation of domestic industries. Industries such as motorcycles,

watches, radio and TV receivers, steel, musical instruments and textiles, where the Japanese had succeeded in developing sufficient competitiveness, were opened up for direct foreign investment in the early stages of liberalization.

Those industries completely liberalized under the 1967–1971 "package" of liberalization were classified as category A industries and allowed foreign ownership up to 100 percent on an automatic approval basis. Industries still considered vulnerable to foreign domination were classified as category B industries, restricted foreign entrants, permitting foreign ownership up to 50 percent with greater foreign equity ownership subject to "case-by-case screening."[14]

In addition, seven groups of industries were designated as "restricted" industries for which automatic approval was to be granted only if the amount of investment per foreign investor was less than 10 percent of the total equity of the firm involved, with aggregate foreign ownership of not more than 15 percent. These groups were agriculture, forestry, and fisheries; petroleum refining and marketing; leather and leather-products manufacturing; manufacturing, marketing, and leasing of electronic computers (including peripheral equipment); data processing; retail trade operations with more than 11 stores; and real estate.

The much-publicized 1967–1971 liberalization program did not, however, open the doors of the Japanese economy very wide because the large number of exceptions and the hidden barriers to capital inflows prevented any significant foreign investment. Furthermore, after the "final" round of liberalization was implemented in August 1971, a series of important events took place in Japan's international economic relations: the devaluation of the U.S. dollar in December 1971 and again in February 1973; a switch of Japan's export drive to Europe from the United States and resultant frictions with the Common Market countries; and a phenomenal rise in the outflow of Japan's direct investments overseas.

Despite the dollar's devaluations, the United States continued to suffer a huge deficit in trade with Japan, contributing to a swelling clamor for protectionism as exemplified by the Burke-Hartke bill. The United States was also irritated by the way Japan procrastinated about removing further restrictions on foreign business operations at home while Japan's direct investments in the United States started to rise.

Japan's industrial sector, whose overseas investments were at stake, finally came to realize the need to reciprocate and began to pressure its government to move toward a complete liberalization, that is, to allow 100 percent equity ownership by foreign firms. As a result, the recommendations made by the Foreign Investment Council along this line were adopted by the government, and another step toward liberalization was taken on May 1, 1973.

The new feature of the latest liberalization program is that 17 industries, including the manufacturing, sale, and rental of computers, will be completely freed from controls according to a timetable extending to May 1, 1976. These industries are mostly R & D-based industries (for example, integrated circuits, computers, data processing, photosensitized materials, electro-medical instruments, and the like), farm and farm-related industries (for example, meat products, tomato products, farm chemicals, animal feed, and fruit beverages), and distribution industries (for example, prepared food, packaging, packaging machinery). The program still contains a list of "restricted" industries, subject as before to case-by-case screening, but the number of such industries has declined. These are primarily industries related to agriculture, forestry, and fisheries; petroleum refining and marketing; leather and leather-products manufacturing; and retail trade operations having more than 11 stores.

Remaining Administrative Barriers
Official regulations concerning foreign business investment in Japan, such as the Foreign Investment Law, are purposely left undefined and unspecific to give greater discretionary power to the authorities. Worse yet for the outsider are the internal ministerial rules and regulations—known as "Naiki"—which govern governmental procedures such as case-by-case screening. Because they are internal, Naiki are not made public; outsiders can only get a feeling of prevailing internal rules through close consultations with officials. Government decisions and instructions pertaining to the screening of foreign investment proposals are practically always com-

municated verbally rather than in writing. Left largely in the dark, foreign
investors have no recourse but to consult the officials in person; this gives
the government a powerful basis for administrative guidance.

Moreover, foreign-affiliated firms in Japan have recently been scrutinized
by the watchful eyes of the Fair Trade Commission (FTC)—the same Commission which has grown so tolerant toward the reunification and merger
movements of domestic firms. One Western critic observed in 1968:

A policy is developing in Japan whereby the Fair Trade Commission is
being given the primary mission of policing foreign companies or foreign-
Japanese joint ventures to prevent them from disrupting existing oligopolistic control of markets. This new mission is a far cry from the original
one which was to guard the consumer against unfair monopolistic practices
of business and industry. The Commission was never comfortable in this
latter mission, for protecting the consumer and policing business was
never the Japanese way of doing things anyway.

. . . The Fair Trade Commission . . . takes on the special role of watchdog
over foreign firms to insure that they do not engage in marketing practices
that would give them a competitive advantage over domestic firms. The
term "unfair practice", in this context, thus becomes defined as anything
which results in competitive advantage to the foreign firm. The stringency
of Japanese anti-trust law is thus seen in its application to foreign firms in
Japan.[15]

In this connection, it is worth noting that consumerism in Japan has recently gained in popularity and political power, and that the government
may be able to use it as an additional excuse for stricter enforcement of
the Anti-Monopoly Law. The Japanese brand of consumer movement, long
in the making with rapidly rising personal incomes, became full-fledged
when successful boycotts were staged in 1970 against color TV sets that
were allegedly priced lower overseas than at home, and against cosmetics,
toiletries, and other consumer goods whose retail prices were effectively
fixed by the makers. Aggressive marketing and advertising campaigns,
often launched by firms affiliated with foreign interests, may be more
carefully scrutinized by the FTC in the name of consumer protection.

Recently the FTC has begun policing technology licensing agreements involving territorial restrictions on exports. Although not empowered to
approve licensing agreements, the FTC has the right to be notified of

licensing agreements under Section 6 of the Anti-Monopoly Law and the right to challenge agreements suspected of containing clauses which are illegal under Section 7 of the Law. Furthermore, an official of the FTC's international section is quoted as saying: "Under the Anti-Monopoly Law guidance for international licensing agreements issued on May 24, 1968, the FTC takes the position that territorial restriction of exports constitutes an act of unfair restriction on business."[16] Since any restrictive clause on exports judged illegal by the FTC will have to be amended before it will be approved, the Commission no doubt has effective power to regulate foreign licensing agreements.

Indeed, it is the FTC that is also actively involved in taking issue with the activities of multinational corporations; it has recently taken the initiative to study the problems that might be caused by foreign-based multinational corporations in Japan and to submit to the OECD a proposal to set up international rules and regulations for the conduct of multinationals.

The Japanese government, hypersensitive to the inflow of foreign capital, periodically surveys the activities of foreign-affiliated enterprises in Japan and publishes studies on them. According to a recent survey, the market shares of foreign-affiliated enterprises in Japan—measured in terms of sales—are still relatively small, although they show a rising trend (Table 4.3). In 1971 they accounted for only 1.5 percent of Japanese industry as a whole, and 3.0 percent of the manufacturing industry in which foreign-affiliated operations are most prevalent. Within the different branches of the manufacturing industry, however, there are some wide variations, ranging from a large share (57.2 percent) of petroleum to a small share (1.2 percent) of food and beverages.

On the whole, the profitability of the manufacturing operations of firms affiliated with foreign countries is far above the average for the entire sector hosting them—and it is on the rapid rise. The index of aftertax profits with 1964 as the base (=100) reached 545 for foreign-affiliated firms in 1970, while that for the entire manufacturing sector stood at 241 in the same year. Many foreign-affiliated firms are showing impressive increases in their net earnings. For example, IBM (Japan) which ranked 16th among the major profit earners in 1969, jumped to 6th place in 1971. The gain of

Table 4.3. Market Shares of Foreign-Affiliated Firms in Sales of Major
Manufacturing Industries

	1964	1965	1966	1967	1968	1969	1970
Food and beverage	0.5	0.6	0.7	0.9	0.9	0.8	1.2
Chemicals	3.3	3.7	3.8	3.9	4.3	4.6	4.9
Pharmaceuticals	6.2	6.7	7.4	8.4	8.0	7.7	8.3
Petroleum	62.2	60.0	58.5	59.6	58.8	58.3	57.2
Rubber products	17.6	17.7	18.8	18.6	19.2	20.3	16.4
Nonferrous metals	4.0	4.8	4.8	4.4	6.0	6.1	5.7
Nonelectric machinery	4.2	4.4	5.7	5.1	5.7	6.0	6.1
Electrical machinery	2.5	2.4	2.9	3.3	3.2	3.3	3.4
Manufacturing industry[a]	2.5	2.5	2.8	2.8	2.8	2.8	3.0
All Industries	1.3	1.4	1.4	1.4	1.4	1.4	1.5

Source: Japanese Ministry of International Trade and Industry, Gaishikei Kigyo no
Dohkoh [Trend of Foreign-Affiliated Firms] (Tokyo: Printing Office, The Ministry
of Finance, 1972).

[a]All other manufacturing sectors not mentioned above are included

earnings in 1970 over the previous year of the 10 largest foreign-affiliated
corporations is shown in Table 4.4. Among other leading profit makers
outside the top 10 were Japan Brunswick, Nippon Univac, Sumitomo 3M,
Lederle (Japan), Max Factor, and First National City Bank (Tokyo
branch).[17]

Foreign business operations in the Japanese market appear highly profitable and seem to become increasingly so as government restrictions are relaxed. Therefore, more foreign capital is likely to be attracted. Yet
administrative guidance and the FTC's interventions may continue to be
used particularly in those 17 industries which the government promises to
free completely for foreign capital investments within the next few years.
Since the R & D-based industries such as integrated circuits, computers,
and data processing are regarded as "infant technology" industries, MITI—
a promoter of Japan's industrial sector—is sure to guard them jealously for
foreign domination. On the other hand, the Ministry of Agriculture is
equally protective of the interests of the domestic farm and farm-related
industries such as meat, tomato products, animal feed, citrus fruit, fruit
juice and the like—what the Ministry, in its modernization program of
Japan's agriculture, regards as "infant growth" industries in need of protection from efficient foreign producers.

Table 4.4. Earnings of Top 10 Foreign-Affiliated Firms in 1970 (in millions of yen)

	1970 Earnings	Gain over 1969 (%)
IBM (Japan)	40,453	62.2
Coca Cola (Japan)	19,635	32.0
National Cash Register (Japan)	8,360	22.3
Nestle (Japan)	8,193	31.3
Nippon Sekiyu Seisei	5,110	209.3
Shell Sekiyu	4,713	270.8
Taito-Pfizer	4,568	37.6
Fuju Xerox	4,086	69.6
Asahi-Dow	3,802	8.0
Upjohn (Japan)	3,668	18.0

Source: "Earnings of Foreign Enterprises in Japan," The Oriental Economist, August 1971.

What is more, foreign manufacturers themselves may not opt for wholly-owned operations, for a variety of reasons, even if they are allowed to do so. For one thing, to go around administrative barriers they certainly need Japanese partners. It is also impractical for foreign manufacturers themselves to deal effectively with Japan's archaic distribution system. In sharp contrast to its highly modernized manufacturing sector, Japan's distribution sector is a labyrinth, consisting mostly of small, family-type establishments.[18] The restrictions that currently remain on the operations of foreign retailers with more than 11 stores is based largely on the government's concern with small-scale enterprises which are vulnerable to the competition of big foreign distributors. Nevertheless, the delayed modernization of this sector is serving, intentionally or unintentionally, as a significant barrier both to the take-over of domestic enterprises by foreign interests and to imports. It is buying time for infant domestic industries to develop competitiveness.

MITI is also preparing legislative actions to revise the Commercial Code with an eye to strengthening individual enterprises against possible take-over by foreign interests. The Stock Transaction Law may also be revised to empower the Minister of Finance to order an injunction against foreign corporate take-overs.[19] Thus more subtle, less apparent, barriers are being erected to cope with the growing trend of direct foreign investments in Japan.

Conduit of Adaptation and Innovation: Research and Development

Creative Adaptation

Although Japan's physical productive capital was bombed to rubble, there remained at the end of World War II a large stock of human capital consisting of industrial skills, knowledge, and experience. This stock of human capital basically constituted Japan's capacity to absorb and adapt modern technology from the West, serving as a major springboard to achieve quick economic recovery and expansion.

As we saw earlier, it was in most cases the Japanese who took the initiative to negotiate technology contracts, and at first licensing was the predominant form of contracts. This attests to the existence of Japan's capacity to absorb and adapt foreign technology without the detailed operational assistance of technology suppliers.

It is interesting to contrast the postwar experience with that of a century ago when Japan, for the first time, embarked upon its ambitious program of industrialization. Lacking local technical manpower, the Meiji government hired a large number of Western technicians and experts to assist in setting up industries. An interesting study made by Koichi Emi reveals that the Ministry of Industrial Affairs—equivalent to MITI in the present times—spent, on the average, as much as 42 percent of its total annual budget for salaries of hired foreigners during the period of 1870-1885.[1] In 1877, the peak year of the employment of foreign experts, the ratio even reached 66.6 percent. Emi succinctly observes: "The important thing to stress was not the large scale investments of material capital in public works and the importation of machinery at the take-off stage, but rather the fact that a large body of technological knowledge was imported in the persons of the hired foreigners who accompanied the new equipment."[2]

In the Meiji era government officials and students were sent abroad. Here, technical knowledge was brought back home stored in the minds of the people who studied in the West. The Japanese government financed all expenses for their studies. It is particularly interesting to note that one of the official regulations issued in December 1870 governing overseas studies stipulated that "the students should refrain from borrowing money or any kind of property from foreigners."[3] This sounds very much like the

postwar official policy for technology imports: "Learn technical knowledge but refrain from depending on foreign capital."

Throughout the Meiji period Japan thus expended a great deal of effort
for educating a core of government officials under the tutelage of invited
foreign experts at home and at various institutions in Western countries.
To be sure, during the postwar occupation period many foreign experts
were dispatched to Japan by the Allied Forces and by various international
organizations to advise on a wide range of technical, social, and economic
problems—but it was not a part of Japan's own scheme of learning from
the West. In fact, Japan did not then take any initiative in this respect.

After Japan regained political independence in 1951, its quest for industrial expansion started. Businessmen and engineers embarked in large
numbers on tours of industrial plants in the United States and Europe to
observe firsthand modern managerial and production techniques—and also
to scan for possible export markets. They were called "shisetsudan" or
"scan-and-examine groups." From those tours, they brought home many
practical ideas and lessons, which they quickly put to use. As in the prewar
years, a large number of Japanese students also went to study in the West,
particularly in the United States.

Important as they were, all these learning efforts through human contacts
in the postwar period served largely to augment, at the margin, an already
existing stock of knowledge rather than to develop basic industrial knowledge from scratch as had been the case in the Meiji period. The uniqueness of postwar technological assimilation was that only minimum personal
guidance from Western suppliers was required for Japanese engineers to
adopt imported technologies and to operate imported capital equipment.

In most instances, indeed, Western firms simply accorded the rights to use
patented or unpatented techniques while supplying only minimum incidental know-how. The Japanese worked out details themselves in adapting
techniques to profitable uses. Moreover, since the Japanese often purchased newly developed techniques even in their rudimentary stages, and
since the type of technology they purchased was mostly research know-
how rather than product know-how, there was a need to perfect them for

commercial uses through further R & D efforts. In fact, it is said that approximately 62 percent of imported technology during the period of 1950–1968 was still in rudimentary stages of development and required further adaptive R & D.[4]

The findings of a government survey published in 1963 revealed how much effort the Japanese exerted to "process" imported technology as compared to the development of indigenous technology. Their adaptive efforts involved two basic activities (1) R & D activity to modify and to perfect imported techniques, and (2) production engineering and the laying out of plant facilities to house new equipment and machinery. As shown in Table 5.1, approximately one-third of the surveyed firms' R & D expenditures were allocated to imported technology. It is also worth noting that, on the whole, the average cost of adapting a unit of imported technology was higher than that of developing a unit of indigenous technology in both areas of adaptive activity.

The survey pointed out that this was due largely to the fact that by comparison with the indigenous innovations, which were mostly simple improvements on existing products and processes, many imported technologies were of a more advanced and drastically different nature, often introducing entirely new products and requiring greater technical adjustments in production facilities—a fact reflected in the enormous

Table 5.1. R & D and Plant Layout Expenditure for New Products and Processes: 1957–1962

	Indigenous technology			Imported technology		
	A	B	A/B	A	B	A/B
R & D	24.9	1,061	0.023	12.8	257	0.049
Plant layout and production engineering	126.6	819	0.154	175.0	279	0.627

Source: Japanese Ministry of International Trade and Industry, Gijutsu Dohkoh Chosa Hohkokusho [Report on the Trend of Technology] (Tokyo: MITI, 1963).

A = Expenditure (in millions of yen)
B = Number of new products and processes

Note: The statistics came from a survey made by the Ministry of International Trade and Industry (MITI) in November, 1962. 1,937 companies were selected for the survey. All the companies with capital assets worth more than 100 million yen were included. The remainder of the sample comprised half of the total number of companies with assets of 50–100 million yen. The rate of response was about 54 percent.

expansion of private investments in producers' equipment as discussed in Chapter 3.

With the spurt of indigenous innovations in more recent years, the above picture no longer represents the present pattern of Japan's innovative process. It does, however, give a glimpse into the past pattern of technological transformation.

International Comparison: Strong Orientation to Commercialism

Japan is among the few industrialized countries which were considered "R & D oriented" by an OECD report published in 1968.[5] Other countries belonging to the same classification were the United States, France, Germany, the Netherlands, Sweden, and the United Kingdom. Canada, Belgium, and Norway were classified as "mediumly R & D oriented," while Austria and Italy as "non-R & D oriented."

With the data provided by OECD, we can assess the relative position of Japan's R & D effort among industrialized countries in the early 1960s. In 1963–1964, the years on which the findings were based, Japan ranked fifth among twelve OECD countries in total R & D expenditures but tenth in per capita allocation as shown in Table 5.2.

Note, however, that Japan ranked second in the number of qualified scientists and engineers engaged in R & D activity. This is all the more remarkable since, according to the same OECD survey, Japan had the lowest percentage of "scientific and technical personnel" in the total labor force as compared with nine other industrial countries.[6] Thus Japan's R & D activity was highly intensive in its use of scientific and technical human resources. Since R & D manpower represents a stock of human capital, Japan's R & D activity may not, after all, be as less capital intensive as it appears. This "manpower intensive" approach in R & D is also consistent with Japan's traditionally group-oriented approach in any business endeavors.

Also discernible in Table 5.2 is the fact that as much as 64.3 percent of Japan's R & D funds came from the private sector—a ratio second only to that of Belgium. Indeed, this is in marked contrast to the case of the United

Table 5.2. Indicators of R & D Efforts in Industrialized OECD Member Countries in 1963–1964

Country		GERD[a] (millions of $ U.S.)	GERD per capita ($ U.S.)	GERD/GNP at market prices (%)	QSAE[b] engaged in R & D (full-time equivalents)		R & D performed in the business sector (%)	Company funds (%)
					Number	Per 10,000 of population		
Japan	1964	1,060	10.9	1.4	197,225	20.3	64.6	64.3
United States	1963–1964	21,075	110.5	3.4	696,500	35.8	66.4	32.0
France	1964	1,650	34.1	1.9	95,574	19.7	49.5	33.1
Germany	1964	1,436	24.6	1.4	105,010	18.0	65.9	56.5
Italy	1963	291	5.7	0.6	30,280	6.0	62.6	61.5
United Kingdom	1964–1965	2,160	39.8	2.3	159,538	29.4	67.3	40.3
Austria	1963	23	3.2	0.3	3,220	4.5	63.5	53.8
Belgium	1963	137	14.7	1.0	15,600	16.8	69.0	64.4
Canada	1963	425	22.5	1.1	23,850	12.6	41.3	33.5
Netherlands	1964	330	27.2	1.9	31,310	25.8	55.5	51.4
Norway	1963	42	11.5	0.7	3,820	10.4	51.7	37.0
Sweden	1964	257	33.5	1.5	16,530	21.6	65.6	47.7

Source: OECD, Gaps in Technology: Analytical Report (Paris: 1970).

[a]Gross National Expenditures on Research and Development

[b]Qualified Scientists and Engineers

States, where R & D efforts were heavily devoted to defense, space, and nuclear fields, and company funds accounted for only 32 percent of total funds.[7] This means that Japanese industry had a comparative advantage in orienting R & D efforts more strongly to industrial and consumer markets, thereby improving its commercial competitiveness both at home and abroad.

To be sure, U.S. military and aerospace R & D did spin off some valuable technical knowledge for commercial application—a U.S. advantage which is often envied by other countries. Nevertheless, the high level of R & D activity supported by the U.S. government might have, at the same time, strained the civilian sector by increasing the demand for scarce R & D resources particularly during the 1950s when federal funds rose more rapidly than did company funds. This danger was pointed out by many observers who were concerned with such a trend. Eli Ginzberg, for instance, observed: "it would be only a slight exaggeration to say that the civilian sector is being 'starved' for research funds, and even more importantly, for research personnel, who are overwhelmingly attracted to the more exciting work on the frontiers of defense and space."[8]

No such problem of R & D resource allocation existed in postwar Japan, however. Just as Japan's economic miracle is partly attributable to its small defense expenditures, the commercial success of its technological progress may be due partly to the relatively small role government played in R & D activity.

Table 5.3 shows that in the early 1960s Japan was far behind the United States in terms of total R & D expenditures expressed as a percentage of GNP, but was slightly ahead of the United States in the comparison of industry-funded R & D expenditures as a percentage of GNP. This comparison, though based upon limited evidence, reveals the pattern of Japan's postwar R & D efforts, which were almost totally industry- and consumer-oriented.

Furthermore, while U.S. firms were often preoccupied with their defense market, Japanese firms were able to concentrate on commercializing the very fruits of U.S. defense and space research. This is best exemplified by

Table 5.3. R & D Funds as Percentage of GNP in United States and Japan, 1961–1962

	United States (1961) (millions of $ U. S.)	Japan (1962) (millions of yen)
R & D funds:		
Government and industry (A)	$ 10,872	¥ 1,794
Industry (B)	4,631	1,786
Gross National Product (C)	518,700	190,040
Ratio of A/C	2.09%	0.94%
Ratio of B/C	0.89%	0.93%

Sources: National Science Foundation, Research and Development in Industry 1961 (Washington: 1963); Japanese Science and Technology Agency, Survey on Science and Technology (Tokyo: 1964).

their success in electronic consumer goods such as transistorized radios, TV sets, and audio- and video-recorders.[9] A prime example is illustrated in a testimony given at U.S. congressional hearings in 1964:

In 1952, Philco had a small contract supported in part by the Navy for the development of a new form of high frequency transistor, which later became the surface barrier transistor. A good deal of company money went along with it, and along about 1953 toward the end of the year, we found we had a working model at the then-unheard-of working frequency of 50 megacycles. The price of that early transistor for military purchase was several hundred dollars each. Later they began to be used in circuits at 30 dollars each, and they went into the computer business in large quantities about four years later at about 3 dollars each. They went into radio receivers about 3 years after that at about 85 cents.

What was management doing during that period? They were waiting out the interval needed for the reduction of the price of a new component. Every manager knows the story: Let the military start it and pay for it when it's at a high price. Let the industrial product, like the computer where the professional buyer will buy what he needs and what he knows he has to have, take the next step. And finally, if you wait long enough, the price will have fallen to the point that you can apply it to consumer goods. In the case of the transistor, there was additional fact that about the same time the U.S.A. price hit 85 cents, the Japanese produced it for 15 cents. The same thing of course has happened to transistorized TV sets at a price that any American would want to pay for it. . . .[10]

Predictably, some Americans were resentful of quick and successful commercial exploitations by the Japanese of U.S. defense and space research results:

. . . while we are spending 'X' billions of dollars or whatever number you care to take for DOD activities for space and space work, particularly in

the case of space activity, essentially all of the scientific information there-
in developed is available to our foreign competitors. . . . I think it's bad
enough to give the Japanese and Germans every bit of technology we develop from NASA that we as taxpayers pay for. . . .[11]

In fact, not only the NASA program but also the global U.S. defense
network actively transmitted high levels of scientific and technical information to the Allies. Daniel L. Spencer revealed this diffusion route in his
study on the effect of an external military presence on technology transfers.[12] According to Spencer, the Military Assistance Program inevitably
involved "a conscious attempt to transfer technology as a part of a definite
policy to build up the capacity of a military ally." Focusing on Japan's
experience, he observed:

As modernization has taken place in the U.S. Army, the upgrading has
been passed on to the Japanese. For example, in the electronics area, the
Japanese had an old family of U.S. radar equipment. When the U.S. Army
standardized a new set, the Japanese received the latter specifications, and
one copy of the equipment. However, in the last few years, they have received very little assistance from the U.S. military in most fields. Only
very sophisticated technology such as fire control on the Nike and Hawk
systems is being borrowed at present.[13]

In the process of assimilating military technologies, not only Japan's aircraft industry was rebuilt and modernized but also all closely related industries were upgraded in their technological capacities.

It is even said that Japan's defense industry has recently acquired a sufficient stock of knowledge to develop much, if not all, sophisticated and
ultramodern defense equipment without foreign technical assistance.
Furthermore, Japan's newly developed defense industry is at present at-
tempting to use its military production skills for civilian applications:

Among those applied are the use of part of the F104 jet fighter-interceptor
building technology to the braking system of the National Railways' super-
express trains and that of the oil-hydraulic system-making technology in
building the F86F planes of the same kind to some fire truck hoses.

. . . Attempts to fully apply such technologies to civilian purposes have
recently started one after another, especially among semi-foreign capitalized or smaller defense equipment makers heavily relying on sporadic
and often faltering defense procurement demands.

Among smaller makers, Japan Aviation Electronics Industry, Ltd. specializing in aircraft gyroscope and connector production has recently started
trying to produce bowling alley equipment and horse race starting line
gates by utilizing its connector-making technology. More significant is its
earlier building of a very accurate seismograph embodying its gyroscope
technology and precise recording of the shocks of the Amchitka nuclear
bomb testing with the seismograph.

Larger makers producing defense equipment as sidelines are more active.
Nissan Motor Co. has started trying out an applied version of its rocket
engine to wind and earthquake resistance testing on skyscrapers and also
to shock resistance checks on its cars in case of collision. Kawasaki Heavy
Industries, Ltd. is studying an application of its defense helicopter
technology.[14]

Another unique feature of Japan's R & D activity is that, whereas in other
industrial countries R & D funds are heavily concentrated in the hands of
several top enterprises, the degree of concentration is comparatively small
in Japan. According to a study made by the Japanese government as shown
in Table 5.4, the top 20 enterprises in Japan, for example, expended 30.4
percent of total research funds in 1966, while their U.S. counterparts spent
57.0 percent in the same year. The concentration ratios are even higher in
West Germany and Italy, reaching 62.3 percent and 72.6 percent, respectively. Japan's small and medium-sized enterprises appear to be relatively
more active in R & D efforts than in any other countries— Japan's electric
machinery industry, in particular, includes a large number of small and
medium-sized firms that are highly active in developing new products and
processes. Indeed, as much as 65 percent of the Japanese firms of this

Table 5.4. Concentration of R & D Efforts in Major Enterprises in Selected
Industrial Countries

		Percentage of concentration of R & D funds		
		In the top four enterprises	In the top eight enterprises	In the top twenty enterprises
Japan	1966	11.4	18.9	30.4
United States	1966	22.0	36.0	57.0
Germany	1965	29.6	43.4	62.3
United Kingdom	1964–1965	25.6	34.0	47.2
France	1963	20.9	30.5	47.7
Italy	1965	47.2	59.7	72.6

Source: Science and Technology Agency, Japanese Government, 1969–Kagaku
Gijutsu Yoran [1969–Manual on Science and Technology] (Tokyo: Printing Office,
the Ministry of Finance, 1969).

class reportedly possess some "unique" products or processes of their own.[15]

From Imitation to Innovation

In the prewar days, Japanese manufacturers used to irritate Western countries by flagrantly copying the latter's products and by marketing shoddy replicas at lower prices. The country-of-origin mark, "made in Japan," was nearly synonymous with both cheapness and poor quality in overseas markets. Although there still have been, admittedly, many instances of infringement on industrial property rights—both alleged and proven— throughout the postwar period, there occurred marked improvements in the overall quality of Japanese products. Here are some intriguing cases of litigation involving infringement charges:

Ronson Products, the British subsidiary of the American firm, which last week won a case in a Japanese court against four firms who had used a patented gas lighter device as well as aped Ronson's design and trade-mark, found that the offending lighters were of reasonably high quality. It has not been unknown for a British manufacturer to complain about a Japanese copy which on examination proved better than its model.[16]

Ikoma Orimono Co. won the second round of a patent battle with Velcro S. A. of Switzerland. The latter filed the suit about five years ago concerning a press-on, pull-apart type of specially-woven cloth fasteners. The Osaka High Court ruled that Ikoma's product is entirely different from the Swiss make both in working principles and efficiency. In clearing the case in favor of Ikoma, the court said Velcro's fastener has been found to be a hook-on type, while Ikoma's of plug-in type with different protrusions. Ikoma's fastener has proven to be six times stronger, further indicating its different character, it added.[17]

This sort of patent litigation has been relatively rare in the postwar period in spite of an ever-increasing number of new products and processes adopted by Japanese industry. This was due partly to the fact that with the relaxation of restrictions on technology imports, Japanese manufacturers found it a good strategy to purchase foreign licenses whenever any risk for encroaching on foreign industrial property rights existed—and particularly when the foreign producers' brand names could be profitably exploited. Indeed, international licensing agreements served as the legitimate system under which the Japanese were able to produce good quality copies with impunity and with great profitability, and eventually to work out different versions or improvements for which separate patents could be secured. For, example, the shipbuilding industry is a case in point:

They built the best foreign machinery under license and quickly applied the most advanced techniques. With strong Government support—the Ship Research Institute is part of the Ministry of Transport—Japanese ship-builders have since improved on many of the designs they previously built under license and now offer the rest of the world the highly effective re-sult of their own original research.[18]

As we saw in Chapter 3, Japan's export competitiveness during the 1950s sprang from a successful assimilation of foreign technology in those indus-tries which enjoyed a favorable expansion of the world demand. In the course of the 1960s, however, Japan began increasingly to turn out indig-enous technologies through its own original research, further spurring export expansion. A recent study made by the Research Division of the Dai-Ichi Kangyo Bank in Tokyo reveals an interesting relationship between Japan's R & D activity and export competitiveness during the 1960s and suggests a strong causal relationship.

The bank's research was patterned after a study made by William Gruber, Dileep Mehta, and Raymond Vernon on a link between exports and re-search effort in the United States[19]—the later revealed that in 1962 the five industries with relatively large "research effort," that is, transportation, electrical machinery, instruments, chemicals, and non-electrical machinery, were also exactly those five industries with the most favorable trade posi-tion as compared with other fourteen industries with relatively small R & D inputs.

Interestingly enough, the bank's study resulted in the identical findings for Japanese industries; as shown in Table 5.5, in 1969 the same five Japanese industries with relatively high research efforts exhibited evidence of much stronger trade competitiveness than did the other eleven industries which were devoted less to R & D. The export ratio and net export ratio of the five R & D active industries were 14.2 percent and 10.5 percent, far ex-ceeding 7.5 percent and 3.6 percent for the rest.

By contrast, back in 1960 the same five industries, although already com-paratively research intensive, were less export-oriented than the eleven

Table 5.5. Japan's R & D Expenses and Export Performance of 16 Industries in 1969 Compared to 1960

A. 1969	R & D		Export Performance	
Industry	Ratio of R & D expenses to sales	Ratio of researchers to total employees	Ratio of export to sales	Ratio of export surplus to sales[a]
Electric machinery	3.26%	1.92%	14.5%	12.7%
Chemicals	2.49	3.07	12.1	4.5
Precision machinery	1.72	1.23	21.2	16.9
Rubber products	1.60	1.10	9.2	8.8
Transport equipment	1.52	0.84	15.2	12.6
Ceramics	1.24	0.57	5.8	5.2
Nonelectric machinery	1.21	0.82	10.2	3.8
Nonferrous metals	0.84	0.94	2.6	−10.2
Iron and steel	0.76	0.59	14.8	13.2
Petroleum & coal products	0.59	1.13	1.2	− 8.3
Pulp and paper	0.41	0.38	2.8	− 0.6
Food	0.35	0.48	1.9	− 2.0
Other manufacturing	0.33	0.41	7.3	3.8
Metal products	0.31	0.26	6.9	6.3
Textiles	0.27	0.22	13.8	12.0
Publishing & printing	0.09	0.15	0.8	− 0.4
Total	1.22	0.92	9.6	5.8
Top five	2.39	1.83	14.2	10.5
Others	0.61	0.47	7.5	3.6
B. 1960				
Total	1.70	0.93	8.9	4.9
Top five	3.33	1.52	8.3	2.6
Others	0.68	0.54	9.3	6.2

Source: Adopted from "DKB's Economic Journal, Oct. 1970, Vol. 1, No. 4," The Japan Economic Journal, Oct. 3, 1972.

[a]Export surplus indicates an excess of export over import

other industries (the former group's export ratio was 8.3 percent while the latter's 9.3 percent) and were less competitive in international trade (the former's net export ratio was 2.6 percent as compared to 6.2 percent for the latter). These findings suggest that in 1960 the current top five research-intensive industries were still in those early stages of the industrial cycle in which the ratio of exports to domestic sales was relatively small, though definitely on the rise. In fact, ten years later they quickly matured into strong export-oriented industries with their relative export share of 46.8 percent exceeding their share of total shipment of 31.7 percent. This development closely follows a pattern of export growth in a follower country consistent with the product cycle theory of trade.[20]

New Crossroads
It is true that Japan has largely caught up with the West in many areas of industrial technology. But how certain is it that Japan is moving to the next phase of technological independence, if not autarky? There are several promising signs that for the first time in its industrial history Japan is indeed reaching the stage of being a technological leader rather than a borrower. Perhaps most important is the fact that in the early 1960s the Japanese realized that they could no longer depend entirely on Western sources for further technological development and began to invest heavily in their own R & D facilities and activities.

Japan's R & D expenditures, expressed as a proportion of GNP, were 1.5 percent in 1969, still much lower than those in the United States (3.0 percent in 1967), the United Kingdom (2.4 percent in 1967), France (2.3 percent in 1967), and West Germany (2.1 percent in 1967).[21] But Japan has been increasing R & D expenditures at a much faster rate than GNP, thereby improving the ratio.[22] In fact, it may be safely conjectured that Japan will soon rank third in the world in terms of total R & D expenditures, next to the United States and the USSR. Again it is worth remembering that Japan's R & D efforts are more heavily devoted to commercial purposes than those of the other two countries.

In recent years Japan's export of industrial technology has been on the rise—a subject to be examined in detail in the following chapter. But it has long been more a buyer than a seller of this modern resource. This is indi-

Table 5.6. Japan's Trade Balance in Technology, 1960–1970 (in millions of U.S. dollars)

Year	A Receipts	B Payments	A/B (%)
1960	2	95	2.4
1961	3	113	2.7
1962	7	114	6.1
1963	7	136	5.1
1964	15	156	9.6
1965	17	167	10.2
1966	19	192	9.9
1967	27	239	11.3
1968	34	314	10.8
1969	46	368	12.5
1970	59	433	13.6

Source: Japanese Science and Technology Agency, Gaikoku Gijutsu Dohnyu Nenji Hohkoku, 1970 [annual Report on Absorption of Foreign Technology, 1970] (Tokyo: Printing Office, The Ministry of Finance, 1972).

cated by its unfavorable balance of technology trade in Table 5.6. Despite a recent expansion of technology exports and an accompanying improvement in the ratio of receipts to payments, the deficit is widening in absolute terms. The "adverse" effect of technology imports on invisible trade accounts is certainly not a negligible factor behind the government's encouragement of indigenous technological progress.

There is also a nationalistic motivation. As I discussed in Chapter 4, there has lately been an "invasion" of big Western, particularly U.S., corporations into booming Japanese markets. Remembering the recent history of U.S. direct investment in Europe, publicized by J.-J. Servan-Schreiber in The American Challenge, businessmen are wary of potential foreign domination of what they continue to regard as infant industries and are eager to have their infant technology protected against foreign investment. There have been myriad official restrictions on foreign ownership of enterprises in Japan. But the recent liberalization policy will gradually internationalize various sectors of the economy by allowing foreign capital to be invested in the hitherto secluded domestic industries. Japanese industry can stem this rising tide of incoming foreign capital to some extent by developing as much indigenous technology as possible to reduce its technological dependence on Western firms. This is indeed a desirable side effect of the present liberalization policy since the major motivation of the Japanese for tie-ups with Western interests has been to secure advanced technology from them.

Strong competitive pressure is also exerted by newly industrialized countries, such as Taiwan, South Korea, and Singapore, which are on the heels of the Japanese economy, rapidly moving into those labor-intensive industries in which Japan has long enjoyed a comparative advantage. As wage rates at home continue to rise, Japan's export competitiveness can only be maintained by raising productivity and upgrading export products. No doubt, the People's Republic of China is a new threat to Japan's traditional areas of exports inasmuch as China's recent detente with the capitalists will encourage its trade in the Western markets. This chasing-up competition from developing countries will motivate Japan to move up to higher levels of industrial and technological sophistication.

Furthermore, the recent appreciation of the yen is instrumental in eliminating marginal enterprises. Over the past years there has been a gradual restructuring of the economy away from small labor-intensive enterprises, clustered in light manufacturing industries, toward more efficient capital-intensive industries. This weeding process, however, was politically painful and did not proceed as far as desired. Undervalued yen had the effect of subsidizing all Japanese exports, but particularly those of labor-intensive products which could compete mainly on the basis of price. The world's currency realignment is clearly another factor which spurs Japan to modernize its industry.

Ironically, recently rising anti-import feelings and protectionism against imports from Japan, notably in the United States, are serving as an additional incentive for the Japanese to produce more sophisticated and higher-priced lines of products, which in turn will make them all the more competitive in world markets. Whenever quotas are imposed by the importing countries or by the Japanese themselves on a "voluntary" basis, Japanese manufacturers will concentrate on producing and exporting high-value products. This has occurred, for instance, in Japan's exports of textiles, steel products, and electronic products.

In addition to these changes in the world economic environment to which Japan must adapt itself, there are also internal pressures at work to make the economy more strongly technology-oriented. Throughout the postwar period economic priority was placed on developing large-scale heavy and chemical industries. Yet the very success of industrialization along this line has brought about myriad problems at home. In the first place, Japanese industry has simply reached the physical limits of expansion by exhausting ideal industrial sites, particularly on the Pacific coasts. Concomitant are the rising social costs of industrial expansion, such as pollution, congestion, and environmental decay, which have been all the more aggravated by the very emphasis placed on the development of heavy and chemical industries.

According to a recent official poll on the Japanese people's concerns about their living conditions, pollution is, as might be expected, on top of the list of social problems.[23] Such a new poll itself is surely an encouraging sign of an increased share of government attention directed to the welfare of the people. For the first time in the postwar period, the people are seriously questioning the desirability of the GNP growthmanship almost blindly pursued by the government.

Pressured by the public opinion, the government has announced its intention to shift the orientation of economic policy from "the pursuit of growth" to "the utilization of growth"—but specific implementations of this policy change still remain to be seen. The 1972 White Paper on Science and Technology, written under the major theme of "new technological challenges and fulfillment," stressed pollution controls, industrial and consumer safety, and natural disaster controls as the new areas to which the nation's research efforts were to be directed. Research activities aimed at these social problems are recently on the rise more rapidly in both the public and private sectors.

For example, the amount of subsidy given by the government to industry specifically to encourage research on pollution controls and industrial and consumer safety jumped from ¥ 87 million in 1970 to ¥ 414 million in 1971, increasing the ratio of this category of research funds to the total research subsidy from 5.3 percent to 20.7 percent. Research expenditures allocated by industry in the same areas also registered an unparalleled increase, rising from ¥ 20.7 million in 1970 to ¥ 33.1 million in 1971.[24]

These research efforts are bearing fruit in the commercial market; the output of air and water antipollution equipment, trash disposal machines, and noise and vibration control equipment rose from ¥ 194,593 million in 1970 to ¥ 348,160 million in 1971[25] —and this surging output is spilling into exports. In fact, Japan's iron and steel industry seems to be becoming the world's leading innovator of pollution control devices:

The Soviet Union, for one, is anxious to purchase Nippon Steel's process of capturing and using the waste gases escaping from basic oxygen furnaces. The NSC process, used by most new steel mills in Japan, converts the poisonous waste gases into boiler fuel or chemical raw materials and also prevents air pollution. It has been sold to companies in Britain and the United States.[26]

National Steel Corporation, for example, has elected to use a traveling hood, made by Japan's Mitsubishi, to draw off fumes as the coke is pushed from the oven. The Mitsubishi hood, which travels from oven to oven, is not perfect, but has higher suction than other such hoods.[27]

A more recent example is the introduction of Honda Motor's CVCC "clean" engine which has been found capable of meeting the emissions standards set by the U.S. Environmental Protection Agency for 1975- and 1976-model cars. United States auto makers rushed to hold talks with Honda for possible business tie-ups, but the Agency suddenly eased the standards by cutting in half its initially proposed minimum life span for catalytic converters from 50,000 miles to 25,000 miles. So far, Ford and Chrysler have reportedly concluded a licensing agreement to produce Honda's CVCC engine. Other Western auto makers are expected to enter into a similar contract very shortly.

Japanese industries, which must operate in the small island nation with a high density of both industry and population, are likely to produce many more such innovations.[28] Of course, preventing pollution is not the only motivation; industrial waste needs to be recycled as much as possible to stretch the supply of energy and raw materials which Japan must import.

Another area in which Japan is quickly developing technological strength is labor-saving devices—an area perhaps least expected for research in such a heavily populated country. Labor shortages do exist in Japan, and they are partly responsible for the development of labor-saving devices. Equally important are increased concerns over industrial safety, which encourage a mechanization of the production processes hazardous for workers. A phenomenal growth of Japan's electronics industry is definitely a plus factor since it can readily supply cybernetic devices required for monitoring and controlling systems. What is more, Japan is noted for its advanced technology of hydraulic equipment. Judging from an increasing number of inquiries from Europe and the USSR, industrial robots may soon become a new export item.[29]

The strongest incentive for stepped-up research is, moreover, created by the Arab oil embargo. Starting in the fiscal year 1974, the Japanese government is launching a massive research effort to develop new energy sources that can substitute for petroleum. Solar, geothermal, and hydrogen energy and synthetic natural gas (gasified coal) are singled out as the most promising energy sources for Japan to develop—hopefully replacing oil by the year 2000.[30] This research project, likened in earnestness to the U.S. Apollo Project, is called the Sunshine Project and will be administered by MITI. The United States has reportedly showed a great interest in the project, proposing a joint research arrangement.[31]

Thus there is every indication that Japan is on the threshold of accelerated technological progress in new directions. Both public and private research efforts are becoming more and more macroeconomic oriented in the sense that they are aimed at solving economy-wide problems. This is a new departure from the past trend—in the 1950s and 1960s the individual firms' research efforts were more narrowly focused on their own internal problems and product improvement. Under the motto, "export or perish," improvements in the quality and variety of Japanese products were often made mainly for the purpose of catering to the high-income consumers in export markets. In this regard, Japan's technological progress has, for the most part, been dedicated to export markets. But it is now the needs of the domestic market and the welfare of its own people that are finally becoming the major concern of Japan's technological development.

6

**Export of Technology
and Direct
Foreign Investment**

New Exports

We saw in Chapter 5 that a great deal of effort was expended by the Japanese to adapt—and in many instances to perfect—imported technology for profitable commercial uses. In the process they introduced many improvements into imported technology and created new discoveries and breakthroughs by their own original research. As a result, the Japanese themselves soon came to export technical know-how. In recent years, the export of this new industrial resource of modern Japanese economy has accelerated.

Indeed, technology exports have been expanding at a much faster rate than commodity exports: over the past five years, for example, technology exports grew to 3.8 times their former volume while commodity exports grew 2.6 times. Total receipts from technology exports in 1971 amounted to $72 million.[1] Although this figure is still small compared to the receipts of other industrialized countries such as the United States and West Germany, it is an encouraging sign; for the first time in its industrial history, Japan is becoming a significant innovator, effacing the stereotype of technology borrower.

Japan began to export technology on a commercial basis as recently as 1950. The trend of Japan's technology exports is shown in Table 6.1. The number of technology transfers equals the number of contracts involving the sale of technology. Hence, one unit of technology contract may contain several related technologies and different types of know-how. In the early 1950s the technology outflow was a trickle; it gathered momentum in the 1960s and turned into a sizable flow with the advent of the 1970s.

In contrast to technology-purchase contracts, which are subject to official screening, no government controls exist over the overseas sale of industrial technology by Japanese firms. Consequently, the government lacks a comparably effective means of gathering information on the outflow of technology. At the moment, the tax credit program for technology exports, administered by MITI, appears to be the most effective mechanism for collecting information. Under the program a technology-exporting firm can deduct from its taxable corporate profits 70 percent of the income earned from technology exports. To qualify for this credit, the firm is required to obtain a tax-credit permit from the Ministry. The information

Table 6.1. Japan's Export of Technology—Number of Agreements, 1950–1971

	1950 to 1954	1955 to 1959	1960 to 1964	1965 to 1968	1969	1970	1971
Electrical machinery	7	21	68	83	78	219	254
Transport equipment	2	3	7	23	43	46	58
Nonelectrical machinery	2	9	19	45	20	50	57
Mining, metallurgy and metals	3	8	22	44	52	131	155
Chemicals	6	15	86	180	143	255	267
Textiles	1	4	9	2	2	13	25
Stone, clay and glass	2	4	3	14	17	8	26
Food processing	1	4	10	9	9	51	62
Others	4	21	49	12	41	88	108
Total	27	89	273	412	405	861	1,012

Sources: The 1950–1963 data came from Japanese Science and Technology Agency, Wagakuni Gijutsuyushutsu no Genjo [The Present Status of Japan's Technology Exports], (Tokyo: 1970); and the 1964–1968 data from Japanese Ministry of International Trade and Industry, Gijutsuyushutsu no Jittai ni tsuite [On the Actual State of Japan's Technology Exports], (Tokyo: 1970). The MITI survey is based on the calendar year, whereas the Japanese Science and Technology Agency's Survey is based on the fiscal year beginning on April 1 and ending on March 31. Hence, the number for 1963 covers only a part of the calendar year. The 1969–1971 data came from Japanese Science and Technology Agency, Kagaku Gijutsu Hakusho [White Paper on Science and Technology] (Tokyo: Printing Office, The Ministry of Finance, 1971 and 1973).

secured from this program, however, may underestimate the volume of current technology exports, since it normally takes a few years before exported technology is profitably exploited in foreign markets and starts to bring home royalties.

Other sources of official data are questionnaires and newspaper accounts. For example, the Science and Technology Agency collected data for the period of 1950–1963 by questionnaire in 1964. Since then, they have been collecting reported cases in the newspapers with follow-up confirmations with the firms involved. Although the significant technology sales are likely to be reported in major newspapers, the statistics thus gathered are inevitably incomplete. But official statistics, though deficient, do provide valuable information on the trend and magnitude of the outflow of technology from Japan.

Aside from the recent surge in Japan's technology exports, changes in the distribution of the countries to which technologies are sold manifest a rapidly rising level of industrial arts in Japan. The changes in the regional shares are indicated in Table 6.2. It is particularly interesting to note that North America and Europe, which had initially absorbed only a small fraction of Japan's technology exports, gradually became important customers. On the other hand, the share of neighboring Asian countries declined from 89.3 percent of total exports in the early 1950s to 28.5 percent in the 1965–1967 period, although technology sales to this region have lately increased again as a consequence of Japan's direct investments. Thus Japan's technologies, initially exported mostly to less-developed Asian countries, were sold in increasing numbers to other advanced countries, particularly to the United States—a trend clearly indicating a rapid technological progress in Japan.

Developing Countries

Although the present share of technology sold to developing countries is no longer as large as in the 1950s, developing countries are still important customers for Japanese technology. Indeed, Japan seems to have a comparative advantage in transferring technology to this group of countries. The Industrial Development and Investment Center of the Republic of

Table 6.2. Japan's Technology Exports by Region (in percentage)

	1950–1954	1955–1959	1960–1964	1965–1967	1971
North America	7.1	6.7	13.3	32.6	30.2[b]
Europe	3.6	10.1	19.5	26.3	21.4
Asia[a]	89.3	65.2	51.3	28.5	39.5
Communist bloc	0.0	0.0	5.4	4.6	4.0
Other	0.0	18.0	10.5	8.0	4.9
Total	100.0	100.0	100.0	100.0	100.0

Sources: The 1950–1967 data are from Japanese Science and Technology Agency, Kagaku Gijutsu Yohran [Manual on Science and Technology] (Tokyo: Printing Office, The Ministry of Finance, 1970). The 1971 figure is from 1973–Kagaku Gijutsu Hakusho [1973–White Paper on Science and Technology] (Tokyo: Printing Office, The Ministry of Finance, 1973).

[a]Including Oceania

[b]Including Latin America

China listed the following number of approved technical cooperation projects in Taiwan in 1952–1970: Japan, 419; United States, 73; all others 39.[2] This indicates that Japan entered into almost five times as many technology contracts with Taiwan as did the United States; by so doing, Japan captured the lion's share (about 76 percent) of Taiwan's import market for technology. Although no comparable data are available, a similar pattern of significant inflows may be observed in South Korea, Hong Kong, Thailand, Malaysia, and Singapore where Japanese direct investments are concentrated.

The Japanese technologies so far exported to developing countries are quite different in nature from those sold to other advanced countries. The latter consist largely of patented, high-level technology generated in research-based industries such as chemicals, pharmaceuticals, and electronics. By comparison, the technologies transferred to less developed countries are not specific in technical nature nor are they the latest innovations; rather they are industrial experiences or general knowledge covering a wide spectrum of productive activities, such as assembly techniques (for example, automobiles, radios, TV sets, and sewing machines); selection, combination, and treatment techniques of materials (for example, dye and paints); machine operation and maintenance techniques (for example, spinning and weaving); training of engineers and operators; designing of plants; installation of machinery and equipment; quality and cost controls; and inventory management.[3]

That is to say, technologies transferred to developing countries are what may be classified as general technology; they are common knowledge, fundamental to the establishment of an industry and different from system-specific and firm-specific technologies designed to give a competitive edge to a given industry or firm.[4] Because of their limited industrial base and technological infrastructure, developing countries lack the capacity to absorb the most modern technologies, which are mostly of a system- or firm-specific variety.

Some Japanese firms complain that developing countries often fail to recognize fully the economic value of industrial knowledge and tend to consider general technology almost free goods or the normal services that should accompany, free of charge, the purchase of plant machinery and equipment. There is some justification for this attitude since most Japanese techniques transferred, such as the skills needed in the manufacture of conventional goods (for example, radios and electric bulbs), are so mature and standardized that they can be readily obtained from any other industrial country. Why is it, then, that the Japanese have been so successful in capturing a large share of the import market for this type of technology in developing countries?

There are many conceivable reasons. Through their incessant endeavors to catch up with the West, the Japanese acquired a great deal of experience and a knack for laying out modern plants, training workers, trouble-shooting technical difficulties, arranging production schedules and quality controls, and performing myriad other production and marketing activities— in short, what may be called modernization skills. It is from this new reservoir of industrial experiences that the Japanese are currently transferring—and will continue to transfer—industrial knowledge to developing countries. The uniqueness of Japan's technological transformation, if any, is that Japan is a latecomer, which itself has succeeded only recently in assimilating Western technologies. Indeed, in this sense, Japan does have unique experiences which should be shared by developing countries.

The process of sharing experiences entails a great deal of personal contact and interaction, since they cannot be easily"packed and sold" in such physical forms as machinery, blueprints, and manuals. So far as the transfer of knowledge to Asian countries is concerned, Japan seems to have an advantage in human contacts over Western countries because sociocultural similarities enhance mutual understanding and communication. For example, Taiwan and South Korea are the two most important users of Japan's capital and technology despite some lingering animosities against its past colonialism. In these countries, there are many industrialists, educated during the colonial era, who not only speak Japanese but are also familiar with the Japanese way of running a business. This is a boon to the Japanese, who are known for their poor linguistic ability.

With the exception of those plants which were set up by foreign interests to produce components for their parent companies, many manufacturing firms in the developing countries must start with inefficient small-scale operations because of a limited local market. In many cases, it is cheaper for developing countries to import than to produce locally, mainly because of the expense of their small-scale operations. Only high tariffs and restrictive quotas can support local production in the short run and fend off imports produced efficiently overseas. Small scale is an inevitable feature of fledgling industries catering to local markets in the developing countries. And there is, without doubt, a great need for managerial and production techniques suitable for small-scale operations.

Japan's economy is noted for its dual structure of small and large firms. Many small firms are highly successful; in fact, they produce more than 70 percent of Japan's exports of light manufactures. Besides, many firms have become large only recently and thus are familiar with small-scale operations. Both the small firms and some of the large ones are equally capable of sharing experiences with the developing countries.

Furthermore, small-scale operations are closely related to labor-intensive methods of production. Most Japanese firms—notably the small ones—are employing relatively more of the labor-intensive techniques adaptable to the developing countries than are Western firms.

The developing countries are also impatient with the slow pace of their economic industrialization. They are eager to find shortcut answers to economic development. Many of them, particularly in Asia, look for lessons in Japan's industrialization experiences partly because of sociocultural similarities, and more importantly, because Japan performed the "miraculous" feat of modernizing its economy, both before and after World War II, over a relatively short span of time.

Thus, looked at in the above light, Japan is in a comparatively favorable position to supply the types of industrial techniques demanded by the developing countries. As I have already pointed out, the technologies sold to them are not specific but rather comprehensive—so much so that technology transfers are in most cases enterprise transfers, requiring the actual participation of the transferors in the production and management of local enterprises for a considerable period of time. There is also undoubtedly a desire on the part of the Japanese to compensate for the relatively low prices paid them for technical assistance services by securing contracts to supply parts, components, and raw materials, and at the same time, participating in both ownership and management in order to share in corporate profits. Joint ventures are consequently the most popular set-up through which technology is transferred.

The manufacturing ventures of Japanese firms in developing countries are, on the average, much smaller than those of their Western counterparts, especially U.S. firms. They are, moreover, generally clustered in relatively labor-intensive industries such as textiles, apparel, footwear, and electrical household appliances—the sectors in which their Western counterparts rarely operate. Even in relatively technology-intensive industries, Japanese ventures are by and large smaller in scale than those of Western firms. Since Japanese direct investment is small-scale, skills are transferred through close human contacts and interactions as much at the grass roots as at the managerial levels of operation. It is said that Japanese engineers and technicians often give more shirt-sleeve guidance in the factories than do their Western counterparts.[5]

In this connection, the Japanese may prove to be an effective skill-transferor to China, which is now determined to absorb modern industrial know-how to implement its fourth five-year economic plan. In fact, China is sending various missions composed of specialists to make surveys of a wide range of Japanese industries, among them shipbuilding, machinery, machine tools, chemical fiber, automobile, food processing, and electronics.[6] Arab nations will also become important customers for Japanese technology as they plow back the oil proceeds into economic development. Japanese firms are most eagerly providing the Arabs with the blueprints.

All in all, although Japan's GNP now ranks third in the world, it is still appropriate to classify Japan as middle advanced, particularly in technological capacity. This status has given the country a unique position in marketing technology. Japan imported the latest techniques from advanced Western countries and exported chiefly their modified or improved versions to the developing countries. Japan's aptitude for turning out improved versions of imported technology is perhaps related to its traditional skill in importing raw materials and exporting finished products.

From Hard to Soft Exports

Japan is now finding more and more that other industrialized countries, including those in the Communist bloc, are important customers for their technology. Predictably, research-intensive industries, such as electric and electronics machinery, chemicals, and transport equipment, are particularly active in selling technologies overseas. These industries have invested a great deal in research activity and have succeeded in establishing themselves as Japan's leading export industries. But many firms in these industries were, until very recently, unwilling to share technical knowledge except with closely affiliated firms at home.

There has lately been a sudden change in the attitude of these manufacturers toward the export of technology. Rather than jealously guarding their patents and know-how from foreign competitors, they now actively promote overseas sales of industrial knowledge. Their rapid accumulation of patents and know-how is no doubt the fundamental reason for their willingness to export technology. Yet the decisive turning point came with their realization that their commodity export drive could no longer be pursued in the face of Japan's huge trade surplus and rising protectionism overseas. As an alternative, they opted for exporting technology, particularly in connection with and in support of their overseas direct investments.

This adaptive strategy is popularly known in Japanese industry as a switch from hard to soft exports. According to a survey made by the Japanese Science and Technology Agency in 1970, some 34 percent of the respondents indicated that technology exports facilitated closer business relationships overseas; 26.5 percent said technology exports were instrumental in increasing their manufactured exports; and 17 percent stated that technology exports were a preferable substitute for commodity exports.[7] If a similar survey were made today, the third statement would probably attract a greater proportion of responses. Technology exports are, however, often complements to, rather than replacements for, commodity exports, since the export of technology often entails the export of plant equipment, parts, and components.

To cite some typical examples of manufacturers who have adopted the soft export strategy:

Hitachi Co. was among the first which decided to make its technology available overseas. Since it organized a special selling force in 1970, it has succeeded in selling some 100 new patent licensing contracts, which, apart from earlier ones, are expected to bring annually about $2.9 million in royalties before the licensed patents expire. Hitachi is already earning about $3.2 million from its outstanding licensing and other technical assistance contracts, twice as large an amount as the level of two years before.[8]

Tokyo Shibaura Electric Co. (Toshiba) organized in August 1972 a new program of training its staff as patent and technology experts overseas and then assigning them as resident representatives abroad. The company has so far concluded licensing agreements for its technology with 80 firms, including 20 foreign concerns. The total number of patents it has licensed is now approximately 200, and the income from royalties and other technical fees is somewhere between $1.6 million and $1.9 million annually.[9]

Mitsui Toatsu Chemicals, Inc., revealed recently that it was going to alter the stress of its export policy from finished products to plant and know-how sales. It had decided to set up a separate company of experts for extending technological guidance to overseas plant operations. Mitsui Toatsu up to now has worked with Toyo Engineering and other affiliates to export ammonia and urea plants to India and the Soviet Union. They feel that if their plant exports increase in the future they will not have enough experts of their own to undertake after-sales service. The separate company to be formed thus will undertake the operation and repairs of plants after they are sold and the training of a staff of experts for assignment on such jobs abroad.[10]

Similar stories are likely to be told by many other Japanese firms. Technology sales are becoming a new important source of corporate income.

Although initially the Japanese mostly exported improved versions of Western technologies, they are now marketing their own original technologies. Notable among their latest innovations are systems technologies. For example, Nippon Iron and Steel Co. recently concluded a contract to sell its computer-controlled production system, called AOL (All-On-Line), to Italy's largest steel company, Italsider. The royalty receipts from this sale are reportedly the largest ever received by a Japanese firm—large enough for Nippon to recoup all the research expenditures it has spent on the system over the past 20 years.[11]

Japan's technology in many industrial sectors has clearly outgrown its infancy; it is well on its way to becoming a significant export. At work behind this new development are two major domestic policies—one pursued at the national level and the other at the company level. The government's new industrial policy of restructuring the economy to a much greater degree toward knowledge-intensive industries by means of its all-out efforts to boost R & D activity is no doubt creating a favorable industrial environment, one conducive to the development of a variety of highly sophisticated technologies. On the other hand, many firms, constrained by environmental concerns and limits to their export expansion, are shifting emphasis from manufacturing to knowledge production as a new corporate strategy. They are setting up separate marketing organizations specifically designed to sell their patents, know-how, and managerial experiences, both at home and overseas.

Interestingly enough, the United States and European countries, which have hitherto purchased Japan's most recent industrial know-how, mostly under licensing agreements, are finding that new supplies of technology are often tied to Japan's manufacturing investments. It is Japan's turn to combine technology with direct foreign investments in Western countries. Yet there is an important difference between Japan's technology-cum-investment strategy and that of its Western counterparts. Western firms had to use the supply of technology as leverage to acquire equity participation because of the Japanese government's restrictions on foreign corporate ownership. In contrast, Western countries provide a very favorable investment climate; the Japanese are practically free to establish wholly-Japanese-owned subsidiaries. In fact, such investments are welcomed in the United States as a plus factor for its balance of payments and employment—many states are, indeed, sending missions to Japan to attract investments. Because they meet with high-wage rates and less-tractable labor unions in the United States, Japanese firms can set up profitably only those manufacturing operations which produce either high-technology, high-value products or uniquely Japanese products at highly-automated but relatively small scales of production.[12] Some examples of the former are Sony Corporation's color TV assembly plant in San Diego, California; Hitachi's magnet plant in Edmore, Michigan; Mitsubishi's synthetic-leather factory in Moonachie, New Jersey; Toyo Bearings Manufacturing Company's factory in

Chicago; and Yoshida Kogyo's zipper factory in Lyndhurst, New Jersey. The investments in typically Japanese products are exemplified by Kikkoman's soy-sauce factory in Walworth, Wisconsin, and Nissin's manufacturing of instant noodles in Los Angeles.

These ventures are designed both to avoid mounting resistance to Japanese imports and to serve directly U.S. markets which might otherwise be cut off by protectionist measures. Thus, by way of direct investments Japanese firms are aiming at retaining—and wherever possible, expanding—the markets they have already secured through exports. Many Japanese firms, having already made substantial inroads into U.S. markets, enjoy well-established distribution channels through which they can readily market locally produced products. In this regard, they are in quite a fortunate position compared with Western manufacturers interested in operating in Japan.

In addition, the Japanese government is encouraging the overseas investment of Japanese firms by legislating favorable tax measures (such as an increase from 10 percent to 30 percent in the amount of tax-deductible loss reserves for investments in advanced countries); furthermore, the revaluation of the yen provided still another financial incentive for overseas ventures since Japanese firms were able to invest an appreciated currency.

On the other hand, those Japanese manufacturers who have been successful in exporting standardized and relatively low-technology products, notably electric machinery and appliances, are seeing their price competitiveness eroded by the appreciation of the yen and by rising wages at home. Since labor costs are a major competitive determinant, these manufacturers are setting up shop in neighboring Asian countries, from which they intend to export to the United States and Europe.[13] Although the migration of labor-intensive industries from Japan to other Asian countries was already in the making around 1968,[14] the trend has been intensified after the successive devaluations of the dollar; Japanese manufacturers found it increasingly difficult to absorb the higher costs caused by these devaluations. Thus they are trying to retain control over their established markets in the United States by resorting to what may be called a circular export strategy—that is, to produce in, and export from, low-wage third-countries.[15]

Japanese automobile manufacturers who have quickly carved out large market shares in the United States are, however, not so fortunate in adapting themselves to the sudden changes in export environment. Since their international competitiveness is derived largely from loyal and highly efficient workers at home and from the benefits of scale economies realized from the rapidly grown domestic markets, they are groping for ways to cope with a decline in their price competitiveness; they are hesitant to start manufacturing in the United States, where the supply of assembly-line workers is unfavorable with respect to both wage and quality; nor are they willing to transplant their production base to low-wage developing countries which lack domestic markets. Although Nissan Motor Co., the producer of Datsun cars, is experimenting with the assembly of trucks at a plant near Los Angeles and expects to open another one in Seattle, its scale is still small, and no such operation is yet specifically planned for passenger cars.

Prospects for Japanese passenger-car assembly operations in the United States may, however, improve with two possible future developments. First, Japanese auto makers will place greater emphasis on style and engineering excellence, particularly emission controls and low gasoline consumption. Rising affluence at home is also increasing the demand for higher-value cars with fancier styles, more comfort features, and better performance. Thus, more sophisticated models necessitated partly by the changing taste of the domestic consumers, and also as a new overseas marketing strategy to avoid a further expansion of unit sales while increasing the dollar volume of exports, will be developed by the Japanese automobile industry. Such an increase in the value-added of their cars is exactly what is needed not only to keep up with rising wage rates at home but also to make their direct operations in the United States economically feasible.

The second favorable development may come from labor-saving technological progress in automobile production. Japan's industrial system is at present highly conducive to automation because of the job security traditionally guaranteed for workers under the custom of lifetime employment, coupled with the current abundance of employment opportunities and workers' growing disposition for leisure. It may be no surprise to find that

highly automated methods of production are more readily and more
quickly introduced in Japan from now on than in the United States. As
the Japanese gain experience with automated production, the feasibility
of their assembly operations in the United States will no doubt be increased.

Indeed, with the development of labor-saving techniques, the Japanese
may even succeed in building steel mills in the United States. The first
Japanese-owned steel-producing plant is already under construction in
Auburn, New York.[16] Other steelmaking investments are reportedly under
discussion between a group of Japanese firms (trading companies and steel
firms) and U.S. scrap dealers.[17] Guaranteed scrap supplies and cheaper
land and electric power are said to be the major attractions for the Japanese partners.

Japan's steel industry is, on the whole, probably the most automated in
the world. Its quick adoption of modern innovations is well known. An example of the export of Nippon Iron and Steel Company's automation system to Italsider has already been cited above. Another Japanese steel firm,
Nippon Kokan K. K., has recently sold its automation know-how to National Steel Corporation of the United States. It is reportedly a completely
automated, continuous type of steel cold-rolling mill, capable of saving
four-fifths of the manpower required for the conventional types. It also
improves yield and the uniform quality of products, achieving more than a
50 percent increase in overall efficiency.[18] The application of these new
automation technologies, and possibly others in the future, will certainly
make Japanese steelmaking investments in the United States more feasible
economically and more competitive.

There is also a unique breed of research-oriented Japanese companies
which are eyeing the U.S. markets not so much for the direct manufacture
of existing products as for the purpose of cultivating the innovation-
conducive atmosphere of the U.S. markets in order to develop new products. One such company, already in operation in the United States, is
Omron R & D Incorporated, Mountain View, California, which is a wholly
owned subsidiary of Omron Tateishi Electronics Company of Japan. The
subsidiary, set up to tap U.S. research brainpower, employs about 200

American scientists and engineers, many of them from firms formerly engaged in the U.S. space program. Among their products are electronic calculators, computer tape drives, and instrumentation recorders.[19]

According to Masataka Tamura, another Japanese company, the Nippon Miniature Bearing Company (NMB), is making good use of the skills and experience of the American engineers and technicians transferred to them when the company purchased a run-down plant previously owned by the Los Angeles Division of SKF Industries, a leading manufacturer of miniature ball bearings and spherical bearings.[20] Unable to install the machinery they intended to ship from Japan because of the Japanese seamen's strike in 1971, NMB was forced to improvise operations, using whatever machinery and labor were available in the United States. They were pleasantly surprised, however, when they "discovered that the engineering experience and manufacturing skill embodied in the machine-man interactions of the U.S. plant were far more relevant to the U.S. operations" than their Japanese counterparts and that "American machinists and technicians could operate the multifunctional machines at much higher speed and precision than their Japanese counterparts." With some adaptation of Japanese methods the company also improved the machine operations, reducing the rejection rate from 30 percent to less than 5 percent.[21]

In another bold move the Japanese are putting up textile mills of their own in the United States, a country that has long been accustomed to the belief that Japan's competitiveness in textiles derives solely from its cheap labor. For example, Toyobo Company, in its joint venture with Rosewood Fabrics of the United States, is building a $15 million dyeing and printing plant near Augusta, Georgia.[22] Many other major Japanese textiles companies are planning similar advances. Their motives are both resource- and market-oriented; easy access to cotton and a quick monitoring of the rapidly changing fashion market. These firms will produce mostly high-value, fashion-oriented products in the United States.

As Chapter 1 has shown, the United States is said to have a comparative advantage of trade in high-technology and high-value products because of its favorable R & D and technology-resource endowments, such as a relatively abundant supply of scientists, engineers, and technicians as well as large affluent domestic markets. This very source of U.S. trade advantage now appears about to be exploited by research-oriented Japanese companies through their direct investments in the United States. These Japanese companies have graduated from the stage of being an outside interceptor of innovations originated in the United States and have moved right into the center of the world's most innovation-conducive market to become innovators themselves.

Thus one characteristic of Japan's manufacturing investments in the United States seems to stand out; their operations are highly intensive in the application of technology and geared to further technological development. Japan's postwar technological progress, which helped it to expand its exports, continues to serve as a competitive factor in the new stage of its economic penetration in the West.

7 Reorientation of National Drive and Priorities

Desire to Surpass the West: Elan Vital of Japanese Industry

Japan's postwar economic expansion has been admired as an economic miracle and praised for the extraordinary growth rates it engendered, a phenomenon that enabled Japan's economy quickly to become the world's third largest. Yet Japan's national income statistics, though quantitatively impressive, do not fully convey the true power of its economic vitality. As the preceding chapters have shown, what the Japanese strove to attain was not so much the growth of output per se as an improved content and mix of output. They have struggled to cast off the old stigma of being shoddy producers and to achieve worldwide reputation as high-quality manufacturers. Indeed, the Japanese have long been, and still are, obsessed with an incessant desire to catch up with and eventually to surpass the West in industrial performance. If there is anything that can be identified as the élan vital of the Japanese economy, it is this obsessive drive to compete with the West.

This peculiar social trait stems from the century-old inferiority complex which has been Japan's since it was forced open for commerce under unequal treaties with the West in the 1850s. As a way to prove to the world that they were a "civilized" people, the Japanese tried feverishly to learn Western ways of living. The Westernization efforts they made in those days are best described by G. B. Sansom:

They made up their minds to take over foreign ways of life not so much because they recognized the absolute merits of Western culture—a point on which in truth they were at that time not able to form a rational judgement—as because the sooner they could display to the world a colourful imitation of Western society, the sooner would the unequal treaties be revised. This was their goal, and much that is obscure in early Meiji history becomes clear when it is looked at in the light of these circumstances. That treaty revision was a controlling factor in the political life of Japan until it was accomplished in 1894 is clear enough from the most cursory study of political documents; but day-to-day social life also reveals, in curious and unexpected ways, how important it was thought by Japanese leaders that their countrymen should make a good impression on the outside world by showing themselves as earnest followers of Western example. Their anxiety sometimes took an extreme form. So thirsty were they for approval that they developed a nervous dread of ridicule. A study of the vernacular newspapers for a few years after 1870 reveals some interesting evidence of this fear of foreign criticism. Such is an announcement in the Nichinichi newspaper at the end of 1871 of an order issued by the Tokyo municipal authorities against nakedness. The writer explains that rikisha men and day-labourers must give up their old comfortable practice of stripping to the loincloth during their exertions. They must cover themselves with some-thing, for the headline says: "You must not be laughed at by foreigners."[1]

Even today the Japanese are highly sensitive to the opinion foreigners have of them and their country. If their modernity is questioned by outsiders, they feel ashamed and quickly try to correct the situation. They even do so simply by anticipating possible criticism. For instance, when they hosted the summer Olympics of 1964, Expo-70, and the winter Olympics of 1972, they went out of their way to "modernize" Tokyo, Osaka, and Sapporo, respectively, by building new highways, subways, monorails, hotels, and other showcase facilities. On these and other occasions in the past, the government has, in fact, capitalized on the Japanese people's in-tense feelings of shame and pride for national purposes.[2]

As anyone familiar with the history of Japan knows, its initial industriali-zation program, starting in 1868, was carried out under the banner of "a prosperous economy and a strong army." This was Japan's nationalized effort to counter the dominance of Western powers. World War II com-pletely dashed its efforts. After a brief period of self-debasement, however, and with the help of fortuitous economic booms, notably the Korean War boom, the Japanese quickly regained self-confidence. Since then, to prove to the world its capacity to create "a prosperous economy," though not with "a strong army", has again become a national obsession. Thus Japan's postwar economic drive should be examined in historical perspective.

During the 1960s Japan overtook England, France, and West Germany, one after another, in the international competition for GNP growthmanship and acquired the status of the world's third largest economy. The Japanese public cheered every time the Japanese government, with the faithful support of the news media, which reported official statistics with eye-catching headlines, dramatized a new success. Industrial expansion became almost a national pastime. The people were ecstatic about the phenomenal increases in the domestic output of iron and steel, ships, automobiles, TV sets, and the like, which were presented in comparison with those in West-ern countries.

Since Japan is a resource-scarce, labor-abundant island nation, its post-war economic policy was, as it had been in the prewar years, aimed at reconstructing its economy as a workshop in the world, importing raw materials and exporting finished goods. "Export or perish" was a national slogan—not an explicit government pronouncement but a generally agreed-upon mode of industrial orientation of the Japanese, who were consciously or subconsciously aware of their country's dependence on overseas raw materials. Furthermore, export performance, once it had become successful, began to serve as a psychological scoreboard for economic performance, as did GNP statistics, recording in a reassuring manner Japan's rising status in the international economic community.

Goods to be shipped overseas were, in general, far more carefully produced and inspected than were goods sold at home. Additional accessories, parts, and safety devices were often installed on export models. This double standard has been acknowledged, for example, by the automobile industry: "Safety standards and exhaust controls of cars produced for sale in Japan are not up to those built for export to the United States."[3]

Indeed, until very recently the phrase "goods for exports" was almost sacrosanct to the workers. They seldom went on strike if contracted delivery of export items was at stake. Aside from the practical reason (making a success out of exports), they were very much interested in how foreigners judged them through the quality of their products. They worked on export products with almost the same competitive spirit and zeal they displayed in participating in the Olympic games. Consequently, the Japanese took unusual pride in their technological accomplishment and export performance.

Viewed in the above light, export markets, it is clear, played a crucial role in motivating the Japanese to improve their products. Indeed, it may not be an exaggeration to say that had it not been for export markets Japanese products would not have attained the high level of quality they exhibit today. Thus Japan's technological progress has been fundamentally "other-directed". The acceptance and popularity of Japan's high-value consumer durables, such as cameras, color TV sets, desk-top calculators, and other electronics products, in the Western markets, especially in the United

States, has not only strengthened Japan's balance-of-payments position but has also served as a psychological booster. Although exports represent only about nine percent of Japan's GNP, their dynamic socio-psychological impact on Japan's industry cannot be overstressed.

Overexertion

President Nixon's dramatic announcement of a new economic policy in August 1971 brought Japan's postwar drive to a sudden halt. The Japanese realized that they had overproved themselves in the international economic game, most excessively in the U.S. market. Understandably enough, the American people's initial admiration of Japan's economic resurgence had turned into fear as they were confronted with the stagnation with inflation and the adverse effects of their chronic international-payment deficit on the value of the dollar. The rapidly increasing share of Japanese exports in the U.S. market and the huge U.S. trade deficit with Japan became political irritants,[4] particularly in the face of Japan's one-sided restrictions on imports and foreign investments at home, which have only partially and sparingly been liberalized in recent years. In the United States, moreover, a trade deficit came to be equated, rightly or wrongly, with a loss of jobs and profits, and imports and overseas manufacturing investments came to be blamed for the problems of unemployment.

In sharp contrast to the U.S. economic predicament was the continued improvement in Japan's economy. Japan's foreign exchange reserves, which stood at about $8 billion on the eve of President Nixon's economic action in August 1971, accumulated quickly in the ensuing months as strong speculation about the imminent revaluation of the yen continued and the Bank of Japan absorbed a flood of dollars. Even after the first formal revaluation of the yen in December 1971, hot money continued to flow in, and trade kept on registering surpluses. At the end of 1972, Japan's official holdings of gold and foreign exchange were on the order of $18 billion.[5]

The Nixon administration's pressure succeeded in forcing Japan to adopt "orderly exports" to the United States and to divert Japan's export drive elsewhere—notably to Europe. Yet this market-diversification strategy quickly aroused strong resentment and clamor for protectionism in Europe. Furthermore, European countries, beset by inflation and the prospect of running trade deficits themselves in the near future, joined forces with the United States in stressing the responsibility of surplus countries to take corrective measures—clearly with an eye to clamping down on Japan's trade surplus. To the Japanese a surplus was a symbol of success and of good financial management, one which they had long strived to attain—yet all of a sudden it turned out to be the target of criticism as unneighborly economic aggression.

In fact, although Japan had dreamed of a resounding victory in international economic competition, it was totally unprepared for such a sudden success in the form of an unexpectedly huge pile of foreign reserves and, moreover, for hostile reactions from the rest of the world. Even now a majority of the Japanese feel that they are poor compared to the Westerners—even though they are aware that they have indeed achieved in large measure what a former minister of trade and industry described as their "century-old dream of catching up with the West."[6]

Disillusionment: Growth Syndrome
Strained economic relations with the West coincided with the rising discontent of the Japanese public with industrial expansion. A large segment of the population began increasingly to question the desirability of continuing such a national drive in the light of the serious problems of pollution, congestion, and decay in their living environment. With their rising levels of income came a rise also in the demand for social goods and services whose provision had long been neglected in the unbalanced postwar economic growth. Japanese workers, noted for their frugality and propensity to save, were frustrated by inflation, expecially by the rising land prices that made it difficult for them to buy their own homes. Thus, despite soaring national incomes, the people began to feel disillusioned with the results of industrial expansion.[7]

The belief that exporting was necessary for their country's survival had been inculcated upon the Japanese. Long hours of hard work, loyalty to their employers, and frugality in their lifestyle were even considered the obligations of people living in such a heavily-populated and resource-poor country. By and large, they constituted a persevering and obedient labor

force—docile by Western standards—and were highly disciplined in their
work habits. These characteristics appeared to be indelible marks of Japan's feudalistic past left on its modern corporate society. Yet their recently attained affluence began to undermine the traditional mores of
self-denial and self-sacrifice, particularly among the young generation
reared in a relatively affluent and democratic postwar period.

The recent series of events—the "Nixon shocks" and the rising antagonism
of the Western countries toward Japan's export drive—caused a decisive
turnaround in the Japanese people's sense of values. All of a sudden they
were awakened to the fundamental changes that had taken place in international economic and political relationships. The maxim "export or perish" abruptly lost all its potency. The government was compelled quickly
to adopt the policy of orderly exports by enforcing restrictions on exports
which were judged to be disrupting other countries' markets with politically undesirable repercussions.

While government officials and industrial leaders went into a huddle to
reassess Japan's economic and political positions, the general public
pressed for the use of more economic resources, including foreign exchange
reserves, to alleviate the social costs of industrial growth and to improve
overhead social capital. The liberalization of import controls, particularly
those on foodstuffs, was demanded as a measure to curb inflation. The
smoldering dissatisfaction of the people with the government's industrial
policy burst into fires of political protest, quickening the end of the administration of former Premier Eisaku Sato, who had held the reins during
the period in which Japan had made its most impressive economic growth.

The subsequent election of Premier Kakuei Tanaka—an unconventional
statesman in many respects—and the unexpectedly great increase of political power by the Communist and Socialist parties in the general elections
of 1972 symbolized the mixed mood of the public, which was in search of
new social values and a new mode of life. Although Tanaka's grandiose
scheme to "reconstruct the Japanese archipelago" presented a refreshing
vision, the public demanded more immediate results in the improvement of
public housing, transportation, sanitation, medical services, and social welfare programs, and above all, in a slowdown of inflation.

On top of all these problems came the Arab oil boycott: it mercilessly laid bare the tenuous foundation of Japan's economic prosperity—a gigantic industrial castle built on the Arabian sand for a large part of its oil supply. Japan has come to realize the need for a more fundamental change in its industrial structure than the simplistic scheme of merely relocating and dispersing industry and population to the countryside and constructing more highways and bullet train networks.

New Challenges
The government was not unaware of the changing desires of the people. This fact is reflected, for example, in the following official statement made in 1970:

A quarter of a century ago, all the factories along the Tokyo Bay shore were destroyed, and although the water in the bay was perfectly clear, the people were cut off from the supply of jobs and food. People wanted food and an income, regardless of what happened to the water in Tokyo Bay. Today storehouses all over Japan are overflowing with rice. Countless companies are looking for employees, while job hunters have decreased. In spite of this the people are not satisfied. They are crying out for a return of clear water and fresh air. It follows, then, that growth is not a matter of blowing more and more air into a balloon, ad infinitum. It must be a sensitive response to the needs of the people.[8]

The same document rationalizes the past policy of neglecting social capital thus:

. . . like countless rivulets eventually joining together to become one large river, small amounts of capital were gathered together to be channeled, in concentration, into growth industries. As a result, the problem has arisen of a relative poverty of social capital such as roads, but priorities in economic development should start with adequate improvement in industrial capital, after which improvement in social capital can be aimed at with the help of industrial capital.[9]

Indeed, this implies that the postwar neglect of social capital and welfare was a part of the growth plan of the government—though not, for obvious reasons, publicized as such.

Yet with the recent turn of events—both at home and overseas, the time has come for the government to redirect its priorities to give greater attention to improvements in the social infrastructure and to the solution of environmental problems. It is, moreover, particularly worried about the

country's image as an underdeveloped society with modern facilities only
in the export industries—and worse still, as a polluting society. Ecological
destruction can no longer remain a regional problem. It has become an international issue, since its externalities are felt across national borders.

Furthermore, the seriousness of pollution and congestion, and the back-
wardness of Japan's distribution system and its social service sector, has
been played up by the foreign news media, with the implication that they
constitute a hidden source of its trade competitiveness. That is, the media
suggest that Japan's exports are partly subsidized by capital that ought
to have been invested in the social infrastructure and in the avoidance of
ecological disruption—and that Japan's imports are unduly restricted by
archaic and inefficient distribution systems. For example, a recent Fortune
article describes the situation as follows:

In a nation that ranks among the top economic powers, only 15 percent
of the homes are connected to sewers. . . .

By stressing exports and stinting on its own social needs, the nation has,
in effect, given away products to the world at low prices—and at the expense of its own people who produced the goods. The Japanese have
worked hard and long, and American consumers, among others, have enjoyed the fruits of their labor. . . .

Official white papers now reflect the view of many discontented Japanese
and meticulously describe the wide disparity between national wealth and
social welfare. It's now openly acknowledged that Japan is a backward
society by many a measure of public well-being, from social-security cov-
erage to public park space.[10]

As the appalling domestic conditions are divulged to the world community, the national sense of shame is once again being stirred up among the
Japanese, and economic policies are forced to turn inward to focus on
these problems. Thus, for the first time in Japan's industrial history, improving the quality of life has become a subject of serious national concern under internal and external pressures. Modernity can no longer be
showcased by simply building monorails, skyscrapers, and high-speed
trains.

Japan is thus confronted with new challenges to "houseclean" its own internal structure and to cater to the needs of its own people; it must create
a truly modern society worthy of its status as the world's leading industrial

state. The national recognition of such needs was no doubt strengthened by the pre-election publicity given Premier Tanaka's plan to remodel the Japanese archipelago, which in turn served to support his election. Japan's innovative efforts are now turned inward and redirected toward the solution of domestic problems and the long-term growth of the economy. The days when the primary motive for innovative activity was to improve the quality of exports have ended.

As earlier chapters have shown, the progress of technology in the postwar period has been characterized by a massive absorption of Western technology and a hodgepodge of improvements, most of them rather fragmentary, made by various segments of the industrial sector. Individual firms have vied fiercely with each other in their struggle to secure, through technological assimilation, a larger market share both at home and abroad in an atmosphere of "excessive competition." No doubt consumers have been the major beneficiary of postwar innovations, especially in those countries where Japan's export drive proved most successful.

Turning inward is also a practical necessity for Japanese industry in the face of the inevitable internationalization of the hitherto protected domestic sector under the recent program liberalizing imports and foreign investments in Japanese industry. Japanese firms must now compete in their own backyards against Western firms for the rising incomes of affluent consumers. Neglect of their own Japanese consumers, evidenced in such practices as a double standard of quality (and price) between export and domestic models, can no longer prevail in an open economy.

In addition to the competition expected from Western firms which set up manufacturing and distribution operations in Japan, rising imports from developing countries are expected to pose threats to Japan's conventional low-technology industries as the preferential tariff program is expanded. To cope with these forces of competition, Japan must keep upgrading its technological capacity to create new industries. New dependable sources of energy must be developed at home. Thus more resources and efforts need to be devoted to the development of science and technology to create an industrial structure that will be truly viable over the long haul in an increasingly integrated world economy.

Invariably, the future direction of Japan's research efforts points to more comprehensive and more coordinated approaches, more central planning. What is at stake is no longer so much individual firms' competitiveness as the long-term viability of the entire Japanese economy. Consequently, the direction of research efforts is changing from private to public, from fragmentary to more comprehensive, from simple to more sophisticated, and from uncoordinated to more centrally organized. It is expected that this new trend will expand the government's role in planning, coordinating, and financing R & D. In fact, such role enlargement is already recognized by government planners:

The right path to innovation in the industrial structure is that of creative development in industry through new technical know-how. Creative development is like a fabric woven laterally by the woof of technological development and encouragement of new industries, and lengthwise by the warp of promotion of wider uses of information, with computer development playing a central role.

Most of such investment in research and development in advanced nations is carried out by government, but . . . in Japan the percentage of government research investment is extremely small. In view of this state of affairs, it will be necessary henceforth vigorously to strengthen the Government's research and development activities, centering on large-scale "vanguard" technology that requires huge expense and in which the risk is great, and on technology which the Government deems necessary to develop without delay, and at the same time to assist development of technology in the private sector.[11]

Research efforts by government and industry are already under way to alleviate the problem of pollution. Other areas competing for an equal share of governmental leadership are the development of new energy sources that can replace petroleum, ocean resources, aircraft, and other high-technology industrial sectors. All these areas involve large sums of expenditure and high risks—hence, inevitable government participation. At present, under the government's direction and with its financial support, "a city of science" is under construction on a ten-thousand-acre site at the foot of Mt. Tsukuba, northwest of Tokyo. A research-centered university and various research institutions, both public and private, are expected to be established. The Japanese are also anxious to have the city serve as the site of a recently proposed United Nations University and have offered a substantial amount of financial assistance.

As the complexities of the problems to be dealt with and the scale of research increase, a systems approach and interdisciplinary team work are required. Here the Japanese may have an advantage, since they can mobilize the devoted efforts of a group of researchers of diverse backgrounds in relative harmony. A strong group orientation is a peculiarly Japanese characteristic. The mores of ringisei—the decision-making system of group consultation and collective responsibility—may prove highly instrumental in systems-focused research activities, since an individual's efforts can be harnessed to that of others for the success of his group's research rather than his own. This is indeed in sharp contrast to the research atmosphere prevailing in the United States, where a general distaste for, and some anti-trust legal constraints on, cooperation among large corporations are said to hinder the effective development of a systems approach in research and development.[12]

With an abundant supply of technically well-educated people, their traditional respect for science and learning, their impetuous passion for anything new, and their tenacity and power of concentration, the Japanese may once again be able to show their innate capacity for meeting, at the national level, the new challenges—the gigantic task of recasting their industrial environment in a new mold and uplifting the quality of their modern life.

8　Some Implications for U.S. Policy on Technology

Technology Effort

The large trade surplus which the United States had enjoyed throughout the postwar period began to dwindle in the late 1960s. In 1971 a merchandise trade deficit of $2.7 billion was recorded for the first time in the postwar period—in fact, it was the first trade deficit since 1888. The deficit was still greater in 1972, reaching $6.8 billion.[1] The sudden erosion of U.S. trade competitiveness in recent years is often attributed in part, if not entirely, to the spread of U.S. technology to Europe and Japan through licensing agreements and the worldwide operations of multinational U.S. corporations. It is even proposed, as a part of the Burke-Hartke bill, that the United States should slow down the outflow of technology to retain a competitive edge for U.S. products.

As has been amply demonstrated in the preceding chapters, Japan has been a most fortunate beneficiary of international transfers of industrial know-how in the postwar period. A study made by Michael Boretsky, a U.S. Department of Commerce senior policy analyst whose work has been frequently used in official trade policy analyses, shows that although the United States enjoys an overall trade surplus in high-technology products such as chemicals, machinery, electronics, autos, aircraft, and scientific instruments, its trade balance with Japan even in this category of products has been running a deficit since 1965.[2] Boretsky argues that the lag in U.S. leadership in high-technology products is a principal cause of the postwar deterioration of the U.S. trade balance.

In view of this recent trade development, some people, particularly those with a strong protectionist sentiment, are likely to reason that since the technology which the United States has given the Japanese has greatly fostered Japanese competitiveness, it is high time that the United States should restrict such a self-destructive practice. Boretsky himself reportedly suggests that as a new trade policy the United States should, in addition to encouraging R & D efforts, "keep American technological know-how at home for a while."[3]

Technology's role as a major determinant of the vitality of the U.S. economy was brought into the national consciousness in 1972 when President Nixon sent Congress the first Presidential message on science and technology, in which he emphasized improving productivity, regaining U.S. technological leadership, and restoring a favorable trade balance through an Experimental Technology Incentive Program (ETIP). The message generated a host of proposals aimed at creating a favorable environment for R & D effort, including tax incentives and the relaxation of antitrust regulations. The enthusiasm thus engendered, however, has withered as key administrative officials interested in the technology effort have left the Administration and as budget cuts have forced the contraction or demise of many of the original plans.[4]

But there are more fundamental reasons for the technology effort's failure to catch the imagination of the American public. People have begun to take a skeptical view of the benefits of science and technology, particularly for industrial progress. Antiwar sentiment developed during the Vietnam war is partly responsible for this trend. Technological progress had, after all, made possible the napalm, defoliation agents, and nerve gas whose use nagged the conscience of many Americans. Increasing awareness of environmental problems was another factor. Modern industrial technology often came to be identified as the villain responsible for ecological disruption and decay in the quality of life.[5]

Not only has the Administration's program to foster technological progress rather fizzled out and the public grown disillusioned with science and technology, but even the business sector appears to be losing interest in R & D programs in general and in the development of new products and processes in particular. According to a survey made by the McGraw-Hill Economics Department in 1973,[6] the R & D effort of U.S. firms will be increasingly aimed at improving existing products or processes rather than finding new ones. The 1973 survey also indicates that U.S. firms expect to perform $21.2 billion worth of research and development, including those sponsored by government, during 1973. The total represents 2.4 percent of industry sales in 1973, a slight decline from the 2.5 percent in 1972. An even further decline is expected by 1976. The survey points out moreover that industry expects only 13 percent of its sales to come from new products in 1976, compared with the 18 percent that it predicted for 1975 in the 1972 survey.

Over a very short span of time the attitudes of the American people, government, and industry thus seem to have shifted from those characterized by positivism to those characterized by negativism. As a result, in the face of relentless technological competition from other industrial countries, the United States appears at the moment to be drifting toward protectionism, even to possible controls of the outflow of new technology.

From Leadership to Partnership

The ever-rising costs of research in the development of new products, as well as its risks, are cited by the McGraw-Hill study as a factor in the recent tendency of U.S. firms to opt for research projects that pay off quickly and that are directed to current marketing and manufacturing requirements rather than venturing on new products. Other factors seem also to be relevant. First of all, the overall consumption of materials in the United States has reached such a high level that new consumer goods can in most cases offer only a small marginal value to the consumer. As the additional attractiveness of new products declines, more advertising and promotional efforts are inevitably required to persuade the consumers to see needs for new products.[7]

Another factor seems to be the result of the experience of the United States as the postwar technological leader in the world market. As we have seen in the preceding chapters, the United States has introduced a variety of new products—first to consumers at home and then to the rest of the world. As the technology gap narrowed, however, the United States began to lose its competitive edge on R & D-based exports. Whatever new products were introduced first in the United States came to be quickly imitated by overseas competitors, and with shrinking time lags. Thus, confronted with the costliness and futility of continuing to introduce new products in an ever-competitive trade environment, many U.S. firms appear to be turning to the defense of existing products.

In the past U.S. firms tended to overemphasize the development of their own innovations and neglected looking for new products or processes developed elsewhere. Consciously or unconsciously they prided themselves on their status as technological leaders and belittled those who followed them. Their R & D program, as well as their corporate reward system, was lopsidedly oriented to innovation rather than to the adoption of technologies developed elsewhere.[8] This attitude probably contributed in part to shortsightedness on the part of U.S. firms, who regarded the sale of their technology to foreign firms as windfall income. Since Europe and Japan have caught up with the United States in industrial technology and consumption, new products and processes originated in Europe and Japan have been adopted by the U.S. market. Thus many U.S. firms have come to appreciate the lucrativeness of being a follower as well as that of being a leader. This reassessment of technological position may be another reason why many U.S. firms economize on R & D expenditures for innovations and seek instead alternative technologies from overseas.

The change in status from dominant technological leader to partner in industrial endeavor may appear degrading inasmuch as the United States has been accustomed to a number-one position throughout the postwar period. But as the United States has revised its political relations with Europe and Japan on the principle of partnership rather than of guardianship, so it must appraise its technological position in the light of new technological development in other industrial countries.

Needless to say, the United States need not resign itself to the erosion of its technological lead in every industrial sector. On the contrary, the United States is likely to continue to excel in such areas as computers, jet aircraft, industrial electronics, and satellite communication. The United States is endowed with favorable research resources and environment, but, as discussed in Chapter 6, multinational foreign firms, particularly those specializing in high-technology products, are investing in the United States to take advantage of the innovation-conducive environment of the U.S. market for their technological viability.

On the other hand, confronted with the rising costs of research in the United States, U.S.-based multinational corporations may increasingly opt to transfer a part of their R & D activities overseas. Some of them are acquiring foreign subsidiaries to take advantage of foreign technical talents.[9] This new trend toward internationalizing the location of industrial R & D is referred to in a remark made by Harvey Brooks, Chairman of the Committee on Science and Public Policy of the National Academy of Sciences:

[The] scientific system is increasingly international, so that the very concept of national superiority in science or technology is obsolescent. It will be harder and harder to tell who is "ahead" or "behind" as frontier science is conducted in multinational institutions like C.E.R.N. and as technology is introduced and diffused by international corporations that will become truly multinational and identify less with particular home countries.[10]

Aside from the internationalization of business operations, the solutions to many of the problems brought about by global economic growth—for example, pollution abatement and conservation of resources—call for international cooperation in research. In addition, the progress of science and technology has itself opened vistas of immense opportunities for the advancement of human welfare in countless areas such as communications, information processing, climatic modification, and space and oceanic exploitation. Many of these technological frontiers are so vast in scope, involving more than one geographic and political unit and requiring large expenditures, that the individual countries may not have a sufficient capacity to take full advantage of modern technology. Thus the future course of modern technology leads to increased international cooperation and thus serves as an integrative force between the individual countries and even between superpowers ideologically at odds with each other.[11]

Social Costs of Technological Competition
Despite increased opportunity for international cooperation in research, interfirm technological competition across national borders at the commercial level is intensifying. As the technology gap lessens, the task of the technology leader grows more difficult. The quickened response of the followers means that the innovator's period of monopolistic profits is shortened. Not only is the life span of the innovator's profits short, but also his workers are subjected to frequent layoffs as he succumbs to foreign competition. The plight of laid off workers in a sophisticated technology is serious; they specialize in a narrow range of industrial skills and, therefore, cannot be easily employed in other industries. Such R & D-based industries as electronics, which are constantly exposed to keen international competition, are examples.

In trade theory benefit of trade is demonstrated when a complete transfer of labor and all other resources occurs between those industries which
contract as a result of import competition and those which expand
through export. How effectively a country can reallocate labor is thus a
crucial factor in international division of labor. In reality, however, it is
difficult to move, say, electronics workers to the chemicals industry even
if the latter expands as a result of export. This difficulty of domestic adjustment increases as the economy becomes more and more concentrated
in technology-based industries, and as international competition intensi-
fies in these fields.

The increased immobility of labor will mean not only a decline in the
overall potential gain from trade but also a greater differential impact of
trade on domestic welfare; entrepreneurs and workers in the import-
injured sectors will suffer more than ever before, whereas those engaged
in the export-expanding sectors will enjoy greater and more prolonged
returns because of higher barriers to entry and the reduced mobility of
resources. This uneven impact of trade may thus further polarize the
protectionists and the free traders, pitting them against each other more
vigorously than before in the formulation of national trade policy.

The plight of human resources in the import-injured firms deserves our
special attention. Human capital invested in the form of education, training, and experience cannot be written off so easily as physical capital,
since once a skilled worker is unemployed over an extended period of
time, his productive service cannot be recouped; it is gone forever. Thus
the disruptive effect of trade on employment in technology-based industries entails incalculable loss to human welfare, both financial and psychological. The social costs of trade that the United States has recently
experienced need to be appreciated by those in other industrialized countries who would follow suit.

Thus, it was no doubt appropriate, as a step in the orderly development
of international trade, for Japan to adopt voluntary export restrictions or
orderly exports for technology-based products such as electronic products and specialty steel in order to avoid abrupt market disruptions in the
United States and Europe. The speed with which imports will penetrate

domestic markets is clearly crucial as a disruptive force, since it affects the importing country's capacity to reallocate resources.

Gains from Technology Trading: Backflow[12]

As John Stuart Mill pointed out in the nineteenth century, the benefit of trade to a nation is not exports but imports. A country gains from international exchange, since it can obtain either foreign products at lower prices or products which are not available at home.[13] This axiom equally, and perhaps more strongly, applies to trade in technology.

In this regard, it is only in recent years that the United States has begun to reap the true benefits of trade in technology with other industrial countries, especially with Japan. Now that other industrial countries have attained technological maturity and considerably increased their R & D efforts, they can be expected to offer more fruits of their own original research to the rest of the world. As we have seen in Chapter 6, Japanese corporations are adopting the soft export strategy, that is, exports of technologies rather than manufactured products. It seems against the interest of U.S. industry to restrict the exchange of technology with Japan at the very time when there is every indication that Japan is becoming more an innovator than an assimilator, and particularly when the interest of U.S. firms in acquiring the technology of other countries is on the rise.

The Japanese, working on technology imported in semifinished form, have produced many significant improvements, as we have seen in Chapter 5. They have also added a variety of highly marketable features to products produced with imported technology. It is worth restating the fact that those Japanese industries, notably chemicals, machinery, and electronics, which were once very dependent upon Western technology, are now the biggest exporters of their own innovations. In a Business Week special report on U.S. technology, a U.S. chemical company executive is quoted as saying: "We are seeing opportunities to buy new technology in Japan that doesn't exist anywhere else."[14] Indeed, the United States, the largest supplier of technology to Japan, is also the largest buyer of Japanese technology. What is more, Japan's latest and most sophisticated technology is almost always exported to the United States even if not to other countries, since U.S. industry can best utilize it.

The "keep-technology-at-home" strategy suggested by some policy makers might have been effective in slowing the catching-up efforts made by other industrial countries if it had been adopted in the 1950s or at the latest in the early 1960s. Since then, however, two significant developments that seem to make such strategy not only ineffective but even detrimental to U.S. industry have occurred in the world economy; first, the technological capabilities of other industrial countries have substantially advanced and now exceed those of the United States in some areas; second, a crisscrossing web of direct overseas investments has been spun over the world market by multinational corporations, initially by those based in the United States but now increasingly by those originating in Europe and Japan.

The first development is responsible for the recent and growing trend of technological exchange between the United States and other countries on a multilateral rather than on the hitherto predominant bilateral basis. More and more technological tie-ups are being made among European countries themselves and between Europe and Japan. If the United States forces export restrictions on technology for commercial reasons, the above trend of multilateral exchanges outside the United States may be accelerated, fostering over the long run much more untractable competitors. Further, other industrial countries may collaborate more closely in research and may even retaliate by withholding the results of their joint efforts.

What is more, the appearance of multinational corporations, as pointed out earlier by Harvey Brooks, may pose a serious problem of defining the country-of-origin of a newly developed technology since an increasing amount of research is conducted within a multinational framework. Besides, if the U.S.-based multinational corporations have a centralized R & D activity at home, any forced retention of newly developed technology in the United States would seriously damage their global operations. Industrial countries are now competing not only through trade but also, and more significantly, through direct manufacturing investments in the world market. Hence, such restriction would probably induce multinational U.S. corporations to transfer their R & D activities to other countries, the result being an erosion of the technological infrastructure of the United States.

There is one interesting, even though little known, characteristic of Japan's imports of technology which is relevant to our present discussion. Surprisingly, Japan has been importing Western technology even when its counterpart is available domestically. Table 8.1 shows the ratios of domestically substitutable foreign technology imported to the total technology imports. One may wonder why so protective a government as the Japanese one ever allows such import competition.

One reason is the existence of fierce infighting among the keiretsu groups, such as Mitsui, Mitsubishi, and Sumitomo, for a larger share in the growing domestic market—a phenomenon referred to earlier in Chapter 4. In fact, so far as the intensity of competition at home is concerned, the notion of Japan, Inc.—a familiar phrase often used to describe the cohesiveness and competitiveness of Japanese industries under the stewardship of the government—is quite misleading, since it may give an erroneous impression that Japanese companies compete only against foreign companies but not among themselves. The fact is that the aggressive behavior of the powerful keiretsu groups overseas indeed reflects their domestic rivalry. Thus the rivalry of the keiretsu groups for the hegemony of the market compels them to purchase foreign technology whenever their rivals have developed or are close to developing new technology or whenever they are able to secure an upper hand over their competitors with foreign technology. The government, favoring such an emulative relationship among the former zaibatsu groups, which were dissolved under the Anti-Monopoly Law of 1947 for the explicit purpose of encouragement of competition, has apparently been quite willing to make alternative

Table 8.1. The Ratio of Domestically Substitutable Foreign Technology to the Total Technology Imported (percentage)

	1965	1966	1967	1968	1969	1970
Manufacturing	49.2	44.2	55.8	68.5	71.8	68.8
Nonelectric machinery	73.0	57.7	84.4	79.1	83.1	81.3
Electric machinery	21.0	32.5	19.8	75.0	76.6	77.6
Metals	46.2	30.3	30.0	51.9	67.5	69.6
Chemicals	37.7	31.5	46.6	47.6	54.8	34.8
Others	61.3	55.8	62.1	75.3	65.4	58.2

Source: Japanese Science and Technology Agency, Gaikoku Gijutsu Dohnyu Nenji Hohkoku [Annual Report on Absorption of Foreign Technology] (Tokyo: Printing Office, The Ministry of Finance, 1968, 1969, and 1970).

supply sources of technology available so that these industrial groups can vie against each other in expanding their facilities through capital investment—thereby fueling the engine of Japan's economic growth.

Many practical reasons also motivated the Japanese to prefer imported technology to domestic substitutes, even if available. Foreign technologies were in many cases superior to their domestic counterparts in efficiency and commercial application largely because of their past production experience. The acquisition of Western technology is frequently accompanied by the privilege of using well-known brand names—not a negligible factor in enlarging the market share of a firm. And no doubt, some export-oriented firms opted for Western technology to avoid the risk of patent infringement or simply to cultivate business connections overseas.

The recent rise in the amount of imported technology for which domestic substitutes are available reflects gradual relaxations of government controls on technology imports—a subject we have examined in Chapter 2. By and large, the domestic substitutes are more available for the less sophisticated, less mature types of imported technologies. Nevertheless, when the substitutability of imported technology is taken into account, it can be seen that the degree of technological dependence of Japan on Western countries has been somewhat exaggerated. If the United States imposes restrictions on technology exports, the keiretsu groups which have vied against each other in importing technology may be led to cooperate with each other in their R & D programs. Indeed, such a tendency seems already in sight as the availability of new Western technology diminishes and the demand for more sophisticated technology grows in Japan.

Local Markets

There seems to be a prevailing view that technology outflows to Japan will inevitably lead to the erosion of U.S. trade competitiveness. As has been set out in Chapter 3, it is true that Japanese exports have been substantially supported by imported technology and that many U.S. manufacturers were, as a result, exposed to serious competition from Japan. But some types of technologies exported are used chiefly in Japanese local markets and do not pose a direct threat to U.S. trade.

One such type of technology is related to Japanese consumer markets. With Japanese personal incomes rising rapidly, Japanese consumer markets are becoming highly lucrative. Moreover, and to the advantage of Western firms, Japanese consumers put an inordinate value on Western brands, reflecting in part some of the characteristics of their recently attained economic affluence. For example, Japanese consumers are willing to pay $27 for Johnnie Walker Black Label. This is an added incentive for Japanese companies to choose Western technology rather than its domestic substitute, even if available, since the former is often accompanied by attractive brand names.

Yet, due partly to different sociocultural factors and partly to government investment restrictions, it is not easy for Western firms to penetrate Japan's booming consumer markets independently. As a consequence, as we have seen in Chapter 4, a large number of joint ventures have been established between Western firms and those Japanese companies which are eager to take advantage of foreign brands as well as unique foreign production processes and product designs. According to an MITI survey made in 1967 of foreign joint ventures in Japan, 129 out of the 327 Japanese partners who responded (or about 40 percent) pointed out that it was an important part of their motives in undertaking joint ventures to "use foreign brands to increase their shares of the domestic markets."[15] In this type of tie-up, imported technology is often of nominal significance, although the use of brands can be interpreted as absorption of "foreign-marketing technology." Perhaps the prime example is the establishment of joint ventures between Japanese firms and such well-known U.S. restaurant franchisers as McDonald's, Kentucky Fried Chicken, Dunkin' Donuts, and others. The rising trend of Japan's imports of technology in local consumer-oriented industries is shown in Table 8.2.

There are many opportunities for U.S. companies to export leisure-related technologies and other local market-oriented know-how to Japan. This type of technology diffusion has little risk of fostering direct competition in world markets. How rapidly some of these markets are develop-

Table 8.2. Japan's Imports of Technology in Local Consumer-Oriented Industries (Class A and Class B contracts)[a]

	1963	1967	1968	1969	1970	1971
Packaging and distribution	25 (12)	32 (7)	47 (19)	40 (16)	43 (5)	68 (1)
Leisure industry	1 (0)	17 (5)	7 (1)	9 (3)	5 (5)	14 (6)
Furniture, cosmetics, and sundries	6 (3)	18 (3)	29 (10)	33 (4)	35 (10)	40 (7)
Dress designs	26 (6)	62 (48)	100 (65)	124 (75)	84 (84)	94 (97)
Total	58 (21)	129 (63)	183 (95)	206 (98)	167 (104)	216 (111)

Source: Japanese Science and Technology Agency, Gaikoku Gijutsu Dohnyu Nenji Hohkoku [Annual Report on Absorption of Foreign Technology] (Tokyo: Printing Office, The Ministry of Finance, 1968, 1969, 1970, and 1971).

[a]Class B contracts are indicated in parenthesis

ing in Japan is well illustrated by an episode in the U.S. maple wood industry; in 1972 it suddenly encountered shortages of wood due to a new demand from Japan, which was experiencing a bowling boom and needed maple for the floors of bowling alleys.[16]

Another type of technology export catering to local needs is in the field of pollution controls. Japan is now acutely beset by the problems of the effluence of its affluent society because of its poor social infrastructure (long neglected in Japan's unbalanced industrialization), its limited geographical size, and its mountain-dominated topography (which forces industrial concentration along the sea coasts). Japan is finally moving to improve public facilities to a degree commensurate with its rising standards of consumption. Table 8.3 indicates Japan's recent purchase of foreign technology in the areas of sewage and refuse disposal systems and pollution controls.

Bargaining Tools for Ownership, Market Control, and Technological Feedback

As already noted in Chapter 4, the sale of technology can be strategically combined with a partial, if not total, acquisition of the capital stocks of aggressive Japanese "adaptors" of Western technology so that the original innovators can share in the long-term growth of the latter. Many Western firms were attracted to growing Japanese markets in the early 1960s. Confronted with government restrictions on foreign corporate ownership, Western firms, notably U.S. firms, began to offer technology on the condi-

Table 8.3. Japan's Imports of Pollution-Control Technology (Class A)

	1963	1964	1965	1966	1967	1968	1969	1970	1971
Sewerage	3	7	7	9	13	8	7	15	28
Trash haul and disposal	4	1	2	1	3	6	9	11	15
Automobile exhaust fume control	0	0	0	0	4	9	5	8	5
Desulfurization	3	5	1	5	6	21	9	16	17
Other pollution controls	—	—	—	—	—	—	—	13	15
Total	10	13	10	15	26	44	30	63	81

Source: Japanese Science and Technology Agency, Gaikoku Gijutsu Dohnyu Nenji Hohkoku [Annual Report on Absorption of Foreign Technology] (Tokyo: Printing Office, The Ministry of Finance, 1968, 1969, 1970, and 1971).

tion that they be permitted to participate in corporate ownership. Although the Japanese government has relaxed investment controls substantially, this technology-cum-investment strategy is still an effective bargaining device for U.S. corporations to use to secure favorable contract terms with Japanese partners.

Legality aside, moreover, the terms of technology contracts can also be designed in such a way to control the marketing activities of Japanese firms which purchase technology. Table 8.4 shows the findings of a study made by the Japanese government on the export market restrictions imposed on the Japanese partners in technology contracts entered into in 1971. The total number of foreign technology contracts approved for that year was 1,546. Thus, the number of contracts surveyed in this table covers 87.7 percent of the total.

It is noteworthy that 75.6 percent of the surveyed contracts are subject to export market restrictions. More significant is the fact that out of 1,026 contracts involving export market restrictions, 749 contracts prohibit the exports of products to the United States.

Indeed, a few years ago, the U.S. Justice Department and the Federal Trade Commission were seeking to block some of these licensing agreements on the grounds that they violated antitrust laws, since foreign firms' competition would be restrained in U.S. markets.[17] Perhaps reflecting the present inclination of the U.S. government to interpret antitrust regulations broadly in order to increase U.S. trade competitiveness, the issue appears to have been somewhat muffled.[18] Although market fixing is no doubt undesirable, since it stifles international competition, one may argue that it is perhaps a lesser evil than outright restrictions on the export of U.S. technology.

Another way of extracting the maximum possible benefit from the sale of technology over the long run is to conclude a cross-licensing agreement. This possibility is rapidly opening up, since many Japanese firms have matured technologically and can develop and exchange technologies to the parties' mutual benefit. Indeed, as discussed in Chapter 5, the Japanese do not just borrow foreign technology. They are extremely adroit in exploit-

Table 8.4. Market Restrictions Imposed on Japanese Partners of Technology Agreements in 1971

	Electrical machinery	Nonelectrical machinery	Metals	Chemicals	Others	Total
No market restriction	62	133	14	62	60	331
Market restriction	138	356	61	186	285	1,026
Agreements with restrictions (percentage of total restrictions)	69.0%	72.8%	81.3%	75.0%	82.6%	75.6%
Market permitted:						
Japan	22	90	25	83	146	366
Japan, S. Korea, Taiwan	4	26	3	12	17	62
Japan, S. E. Asia	24	164	13	43	83	327
Japan, S. E. Asia, Europe	10	3	0	1	0	14
Any country except the Communist bloc	6	14	0	14	4	38
Others	72	59	20	33	35	219
Total	200	489	75	248	345	1,357

Source: Japanese Science and Technology Agency, Gaikoku Gijutsu Dohnyu Nenji Hohkoku [Annual Report on Absorption of Foreign Technology] (Tokyo: Printing Office, The Ministry of Finance, 1973).

ing new scientific discoveries for quick commercial applications, best exemplified by the successful commercialization of the Wankel rotary engine by Toyo Kogyo. Under a cross-licensing agreement the suppliers of the original technology are sure to benefit whenever the Japanese licensees produce improvements.

The rising interest of Western companies in capitalizing on Japan's present, as well as potential, technological capability is reflected in the increase in recent years of cross-licensing agreements, which did not exist until 1963. Joint R & D contracts also are being signed. This trend (Table 8.5) augurs the advent of the new era of technological relationship between Japan and Western countries.

Meeting the Challenge

In the face of stiffened technological competition in the world market U.S. firms are no longer giving away technology to potential foreign competitors. They are not only extremely tactical in arranging the sale of technology, but also are resorting to strategies such as technology-cum-investment, export market restrictions, and cross-licensing, to prolong returns on it, as we have seen above.

Restrictions are thus already being imposed by individual U.S. firms on their overseas sale of technology—not negatively, to obstruct the exchange of industrial knowledge, as envisaged in the keep-technology-at-home scheme, but positively, to secure as much benefit as possible from the sale of technology through the market mechanism. Agreements are made in such a way as to benefit from the future growth and technological progress of other countries. So far as the gains from technology trade are concerned, the adaptive approach of the individual firm is certainly far superior to the protectionist solution of imposing official controls on technology outflows.

One may still argue, however, that even if the profits of the individual firm can be maximized by a variety of new tactical strategies, the problems confronting U.S. workers remain unsolved and may even become more serious as jobs are continually exported, together with technology. How can the United States cope with this negative employment effect?

Table 8.5. Cross Licensing Agreements and Joint R & D Contracts between Japanese and Foreign Firms

Number of cross licensing agreements, both Class A and Class B, including joint R & D contracts (the figure in parentheses indicates the number of joint R & D)

	1963	1964	1965	1966	1967	1968	1969	1970	1971
Nonelectric machinery				1	7 (1)	4 (3)	5 (2)	3	11 (2)
Electric machinery		1	1	2	3	17	8	10	25
Metals and metal products				4 (1)		2(1)		2	4
Chemicals	1		1	1	9 (1)	12	8	4	12 (3)
Others			1	1		6		7	2
Total	1	1	3	8 (1)	19 (2)	40 (4)	21 (2)	26	54 (5)

Source: Japanese Science and Technology Agency, Gaikoku Gijutsu Dohnyu Nenji Hohkoku [Annual Report on Absorption of Foreign Technology] (Tokyo: Printing Office, The Ministry of Finance, 1969, 1971, 1972, and 1973).

Technology inflows from other countries are obviously beneficial to U.S. workers. These inflows raise the productive efficiency and competitiveness of U.S. firms. At the macroeconomic level, technological stimuli thus imported encourage domestic investment, which in turn raises aggregate demand and creates more employment opportunities. As more and more new technologies are generated overseas, the United States can benefit from technology trading as do other countries. Yet the United States still has a huge surplus in technology trading. This implies that so far as the employment effect of technology trading is concerned, the United States is not gaining as much as the rest of the world is. Technologies imported by the United States are, moreover, normally of the most sophisticated types, those which supplement the growth of high-technology industries—more intensive in the use of capital and skills and more automated.

The negative employment effect is probably felt most severely by the less skilled. For the United States has lost and will continue to lose trade competitiveness in relatively unsophisticated segments of technology-based industries. To prolong whatever advantages remain—technical know-how, managerial experience, marketing networks and the like—U.S. firms in those declining sectors often resort to overseas production, that is, setting up factories in other countries or licensing foreign producers.

Meanwhile, U.S. trade advantage in manufactures is increasingly concentrated in narrow fields of high-technology industries demanding a highly skilled labor force. The net result is an increasing qualitative gap between the demand for and the supply of labor. Since the interests of less skilled workers are by and large represented by labor unions, political pressure will be exerted to protect the declining industries from imports as well as from transfers of technology. In this connection the following incisive observation made by James C. Abegglen and William V. Rapp, which compares trade policies between the United States and Japan, is relevant:

The important fact about trade policy is not that one or the other nation is protectionist; the two nations appear now to be about equally "free-trading," although the trend lines are diverging. The important fact is that Japan, with a coherent and economically rational industrial policy, is protecting her high technology, high growth sectors while the protectionism of the United States is directed to the low growth, low technology sectors. It is evident, and will be . . . that these respective positions tend to accelerate Japan's growth and hence her international competitiveness while depressing U.S. growth and competitive capability.[19]

The pressure for an industrial structural shift brought about by changing world economic conditions is providing an opportunity for U.S. labor to specialize more than formerly in high-productivity, high-paying occupations. But to take advantage of this opportunity, new industries must be created and the overall level of labor skills needs to be upgraded. More retraining of workers and assistance to firms in the declining sectors is required. The present adjustment assistance program certainly should be expanded substantially to cushion the impact of technological competition. At the same time, greater human motivations to capitalize on better opportunities at an individual's level and foresighted leadership at the national level are called for to meet the new challenges posed by changing international economic and technological relations. The public's faith in and enthusiam for science and technology must be restored. In short, there is definitely a need for the United States to revitalize its technology effort.

Considering the rapid rise of technology trading with Japan, should the United States impose controls? The foregoing analysis seems to indicate that it should not. Japan's technological progress is no longer one-sidedly dependent on Western technology. As previous chapters have shown, Japan is quickly catching up with Western countries in R & D efforts and has proved to be an effective innovator in many industrial sectors. The United States can neither stop the momentum of technological progress in Japan nor win technological competition by simply curbing technology outflows. Such an approach is defeatist. The diffusion of the U.S. technology, which has helped Japan attain its current status—since it is irreversible—should be considered an investment. And the United States should seek dividends from the growth of the Japanese economy and technological advance by expanding trade in manufactures, technology, and direct investments.

A recent report of one of the United States' responses to the energy crisis provides a hopeful sign. The United States has expressed interest in signing an agreement for cooperation in research on the Sunshine Project, Japan's research program which is directed at the development of new sources of energy other than oil, described in Chapter 5. This would indeed be a constructive and promising approach. Such a joint effort could help avert competitive scrambles for oil and provide a basis for a strong and lasting entente between two countries whose economic relationship has been on tenterhooks more often than not in the recent past. And finally, the strategies recently employed by U.S. firms in their technology exports and the new insistence of the U.S. government on the liberalization of imports and direct investments in Japan should provide a basis for more rational trade relations between these two nations.

Appendix

Notes on the "MITI-License Survey"

Chapter 3 relies on the data collected and published by the Japanese Ministry of International Trade and Industry in Gaikoku Gijutsu Donyu no Genjo to Mondaiten (Current Status and Problems of Foreign Technology Absorption) (Tokyo: MITI, 1962). The data was compiled from a survey made by sending questionnaires to all the technology-importing companies in August 1961. The survey covered the category A licensing agreements which were concluded during the period from June 1950 to March 1961.

1
The coverage of the survey:

Number of companies which acquired foreign technology from June 1950 to March 1961	Number of technology-importing companies responding to the survey	Rate of response
610	470	77.0%

Number of licensing agreements (category A) concluded from June 1950 to March 1961	Number of licensing agreements covered by the survey	Rate of response
1,396	1,230	88.3%

About 30 companies out of 610 companies which imported technology went bankrupt or merged with other companies prior to the survey. Consequently, the actual number of technology-importing companies existing at the time of the survey was approximately 580. Hence the actual rate of response can be considered higher than 77 percent.

The total royalty payments reported in the survey amounted to ¥121,104 million before taxes. The total royalty payments reported separately by the Bank of Japan was ¥110,098 million after taxes. Assuming an average tax rate of 15 percent, the former corresponded to 93.5 percent of the latter. Thus, the survey had a high degree of representation.

2
Estimation of imported-technology-based products: In order to avoid double counting, the value of imported-technology-based products was

counted only once, at their primary stage of manufacturing, and was estimated at the factory delivery price. Those imported-technology-based products which were consumed internally or which were kept in inventory were also included in the estimation. When a foreign license was related to an intermediate process of production, the value added by that process was estimated. For example, the value of textiles that contained synthetic fibers produced with imported technology was estimated at the factory delivery price from the chemical industry. If a further processing using foreign technology was involved in making the synthetic fabrics, an additional estimate was made of the value added component associated with such processing in the textile industry.

The export value of imported-technology-based products includes that of those imported-technology-based products which were purchased by domestic producers and used as inputs in the export sector. For example, if transistors were used as an intermediate input for exported communications equipment, the value of the transistors alone was calculated at the factory delivery price. All in all, the value of imported-technology-based products somewhat overestimates the contribution made by foreign technology, since the contributions made by various supplementary and complementary technologies developed in Japan are not fully taken account of.

The Ministry provides no explanation to the method of collecting figures on imported-technology-based investment (that is, investment directly associated with imported technology). We assume that these figures were subjectively estimated by the businessmen who responded to the survey.

These data are doubtless marred by many errors, omissions, and arbitrary estimations. This was the first survey on licensing operations carried out by the Ministry. Nevertheless, Japanese data on technology is generally of high quality because of the Government's interest in the matter. For example, data on research and development is said to be comparable in quality to that of the United States. According to the OECD: "For the United States and Japan the available statistics represent a major systematic effort over several years; for some other countries the element of guesswork is still too large": Organization for Economic Co-operation and Development, <u>Science, Economic Growth and Government Policy</u>, Paris 1963, p. 93.

Notes

Chapter 1

1

Economic Planning Agency, Japanese Government, Economic Survey of Japan—1970–1971 (Tokyo: The Japan Times, 1972), p. 72.

2

Joseph A. Schumpeter, Capitalism, Socialism and Democracy (New York: Harper & Row, 1950), p. 31.

3

John J. Murphy defines the concept of technology at three levels: "The simplest version views technology as involving only changes in artifacts. A more sophisticated approach adds to the physical objects, labor and managerial skills. This approach is susceptible to aggregate analysis, and economic theorists and historians have made wide use of it. A third approach views technology as a 'socio-technological' phenomenon, that is, besides involving material and artifact improvements, technology is considered to incorporate a cultural, social, and psychological process as well. In this view any detail of change, if it is to be effective and if the ultimate repercussions are to be anticipated, must be related to the 'central values of the culture'." The third approach, which Murphy saw in the works of anthropologists such as George M. Foster and Margaret Mead, is essential for interpreting the Japanese case. See J. J. Murphy, "Retrospect and Prospect," in Daniel L. Spencer and Alexander Woroniak, eds., The Transfer of Technology to Developing Countries (New York: Praeger, © 1967), pp. 6–7.

4

Joseph A. Schumpeter, The Theory of Economic Development (New York: Oxford University Press, 1961), Chapters 2 and 6.

5

Ibid., p. 68.

6

Kenneth K. Kurihara, The Growth Potential of the Japanese Economy (Baltimore: The Johns Hopkins Press, 1971), pp. 3–4.

7

Schumpeter, Economic Development, pp. 95–127.

8

See, for example, Kurihara, Japanese Economy, p. 75.

9

Leon Hollerman, "Recent Difficulties in Japan's Economic Development," Banca Nazionale del Lavoro Quarterly Review, N. 88 (March 1969), p. 5.

10

The close relationship between government and business was no doubt an important factor in reducing the risk associated with overinvestment. See James C. Abegglen and William V. Rapp, "Japanese Managerial Behavior and 'Excessive Competition'," The Developing Economies, Vol. 8, No. 4 (December 1970), pp. 427–444.

11

The petrochemical industry provides a good example of excess capacity created by investment rather than by stagnated demand. The Petrochemical Equipment Coordinating Council, composed of petrochemical manufacturers and MITI, recently made a decision to suspend any new equipment expansion in almost all major branches of the industry until the end of 1974. The decision constitutes a truce for the equipment expansion race, which had created a huge excess capacity within the industry. Even with the suspension of investment, it was expected that the operation rate would not reach 90 percent of the break-even point. See The Japan Economic Journal, September 19, 1972. This example clearly illustrates the important role the government plays in guiding the private sector's decisions of investment.

12

For an analysis of the dual industrial structure, see Seymour Broadbridge, Industrial Dualism in Japan (Chicago: Aldine Co., 1966).

13

Raymond Vernon incorporated the concept of product life cycle into a trade model in "International Investment and International Trade in the Product Life Cycle," Quarterly Journal of Economics, Vol. LXXX (May 1966), pp. 190–207. For an excellent survey of the theory, see Louis T. Wells, Jr., "International Trade: The Product Life Cycle Approach," in The Product Life Cycle and International Trade, edited by him (Boston: Division of Research, Graduate School of Business Administration, Harvard University, 1972), pp. 3–38.

14

Strong causative effects in the United States of R & D activity and the abundance of labor skills on trade competitiveness were suggested by Donald B. Keesing in "The Impact of Research and Development on United States Trade," Journal of Political Economy, LXXV (February 1967) pp. 38–48; "Labor Skills and International Trade: Evaluating Many Trade Flows with a Single Measuring Device," Review of Economics and Statistics, XLVII (August 1965) pp. 287–294; "Labor Skills and Comparative Advantage," American Economic Review Proceedings, LVI (May 1966) pp. 249–258. Keesing's findings are all consistent with and supportive of the neotechnology approach.

15

The hypothesis that similar demand structures (or similar per capita incomes) between countries constitute the basis of trade in manufactures was advanced by Staffan Burenstam Linder in An Essay on Trade and Transformation (Stockholm: Almqvist & Wiksell, 1961).

16

This diffusion process involves what may be called a "metamorphic effect" on the overseas earnings of the United States accruable from new products. During the early period of the product life cycle of a new product, when the United States enjoys an advantage, export earnings, a positive item on the merchandise account of its balance of payments, are generated. Later, as the production of the new product spreads to other countries, foreign demands are gradually satisfied overseas by local production, which results in a slowdown and, eventually, a decline in U.S. export of the new product. As discussed above, during this dissemination period the original U.S. manufacturer itself may participate actively in the foreign production of the new product by supplying technology and capital; in this case, the resulting capital outflow constitutes a negative item on the capital account of the U.S. balance of payments. With a subsequent foreign production, however, dividends, royalties, and management fees start to flow in as a new source of revenues, in addition to items on the invisible trade account.

In short, expressed in terms of the Hagel–Schumpeterian dialectical logic, technology-based exports from the United States are often predestined to destroy themselves by virtue of their own success and to metamorphose from merchandise trade transactions into invisible trade transactions. See my essay, "Imitation, Innovation, and Japanese Exports," in Peter B. Kenen and Roger Lawrence, eds., The Open Economy: Essays on International Trade and Finance (New York: Columbia University Press, 1968), p. 198; and Frank S. Wert, "U.S.-Based Multinationalism. A Conceptual Analysis" (Ph.D. dissertation, Colorado State University, 1972), Chapter IV. The latter elaborates on my theme.

17
On this point, see William Gruber, Dileep Mehta, and Raymond Vernon, "The R & D Factor in International Trade and International Investment of United States Industries," The Journal of Political Economy, Vol. 75, No. 1 (February 1967). They state that "One way of looking at the overseas direct investments of U.S. producers of manufactures is that they are the final step in a process which begins with the involvement of such producers in export trade. The export trade of the United States . . . is heavily weighted with products that demand large scientific and technical inputs in the selling process. Products of this sort . . . ordinarily demand an apparatus for learning customer needs and for subsequent technical servicing and consulting. Once such an organization has been established for sales purposes, the marginal costs of setting up a facility for production may be sharply reduced . . ." (p. 30).

18
Stephen Hymer, "International Operations of National Firms—A Study of Direct Foreign Investment" (Ph.D. dissertation, Massachusetts Institute of Technology, 1960).

19
James C. Abegglen and William V. Rapp, "The Competitive Impact of Japanese Growth," in Jerome B. Cohen, ed., Pacific Partnership: United

States–Japan Trade (Lexington, Mass.: D.C. Heath & Co., 1972), pp. 19–50.

20

The liberalization of direct foreign investments in Japan is discussed in Chapter 4.

21

The Japan Chamber of Commerce, "A Survey on the Degree of Interest of Japanese Manufacturers in Overseas Ventures" (mimeographed, Tokyo: The Japan Chamber of Commerce, 1971).

22

"Trading Houses in Japan," The Oriental Economist, January 1970, p. 38.

23

They are particularly active in overseas investments to exploit natural resources, iron ore, coal, petroleum, and other industrial resources.

24

For investment activities of trading firms, see Terutomo Ozawa, Transfer of Technology from Japan to Developing Countries, UNITAR Research Report No. 7 (New York: UNITAR, 1970), pp. 31–35.

25

Terutomo Ozawa, "Multinationalism, Japanese Style," Columbia Journal of World Business, Vol. 7, No. 6 (November–December 1972), p. 40.

26

The Japan Economic Journal September 19, 1972. It should be noted that these forward-looking strategies are espoused by MITI against some objections of the Ministry of Agriculture. The former, for example, strongly advocates the liberalization of agricultural imports for better resource reallocation, whereas the latter is adamant on protecting such sectors as citrus and dairy farms.

27

The Japan Economic Journal, May 23, 1972.

28

Nihon Keizai Shimbun, February 29, 1972.

29

This new strategy is discussed in Chapter 6.

30

Arnold J. Toynbee, A Study of History (New York: Oxford University Press, 1962), pp. 271–338.

31

The following observation is pertinent: "Statements that countries well endowed with skills will export skill-intensive products are no different from and no more illuminating than statements that countries well endowed with machines will tend to export machine-intensive goods. The fixed-endowment factor box used in every trade course helps us to describe national endowments and the two-way trade flows that endowments gen-

erate, but it is inadequate for a long-run analysis. It does not tell us how endowments come into being and why they should differ between countries." Peter B. Kenen, "Skills, Human Capital, and Comparative Advantage," in W. L. Hansen, ed., Education, Income, and Human Capital (New York: National Bureau of Economic Research, 1970), p. 206.
32
Charles P. Kindleberger, Foreign Trade and the National Economy (New Haven: Yale University Press, 1964), p. 99.

Chapter 2
1
William W. Lockwood, "Political Economy," in Herbert Passin, ed., The United States and Japan (Englewood, N.J.: Prentice-Hall, © 1966), p. 103.
2
A full English text of the law was published by Industrial Bank of Japan, Law Concerning Foreign Investment, the Regulation Relating to the Enforcement of the Law Concerning Foreign Investment, and Foreign Investment Commission Establishment Law (October 1950).
3
The full text of his speech is reproduced by the Ministry of Finance, Japanese Government, A Guide to Investment in Japan (Tokyo, 1950).
4
This type of announcement was required by the Foreign Investment Law, in which Article 7–1 stipulates: "The Minister of Finance and the Minister of International Trade and Industry shall, in accordance with the Ministry of Finance Ordinance and the Ministry of International Trade and Industry Ordinance, make public a list of the kinds of technologies concerned with technological assistance from foreign investors is desired." See Industrial Bank of Japan, Law Concerning Foreign Investment.
5
For a detailed analysis of how the balance of payments difficulties constituted the major bottleneck to the economic growth in Japan, see Leon Hollerman, Japan's Dependence on the World Economy: The Approach Toward Economic Liberalization (Princeton, N.J.: Princeton University Press, 1967), pp. 174–185.
6
Quoted in "Liking for Licensing," Chemical Week (May 30, 1964), p. 55.
7
"Industrial Innovation Boom," The Oriental Economist, February 1957, p. 74.
8
The group visited the Far East under the auspices of the London and Birmingham Chambers of Commerce in 1965. Part of their report is quoted

by Richard Bullard, in "There's Business Waiting To Be Won in the Far East," Commerce, Journal of the London Chamber of Commerce, May 1965, p. 14.
9
Albert O. Hirschman, "Effects of Industrialization on the Markets of Industrial Countries," in Bert F. Hoselitz, ed., The Progress of Underdeveloped Areas (Chicago: University of Chicago Press, 1952), pp. 270-283.
10
During the postwar period of 1945-1968, U.S. firms originated about 60 percent of 110 major innovations, and European firms, including Canada and Japan, about 38 percent. See OECD, Gaps in Technology: Analytical Report (Paris: 1970), p. 185.
11
National Industrial Conference Board, Foreign Licensing Agreements, Studies in Business Policy, No. 91 (New York: 1960), p. 66.
12
Daniel Hamberg, Essays on the Economics of Research and Development (New York: Random House, © 1966), p. 11.
13
Ibid.
14
James C. Abegglen, ed., Business Strategies for Japan (Tokyo: Sophia University Press, 1970), p. 125.
15
This structural shift may be desirable from the entrepreneur's standpoint, but it creates a serious problem for U.S. labor, particularly the unskilled. This aspect of the resource-reallocation problems of the U.S. economy is discussed in Chapter 8.
16
On this point, see Daniel L. Spencer, Technology Gap in Perspective (New York: Spartan Books, 1970), pp. 41-44.

Chapter 3
1
This export-as-residual view is emphasized by Staffan Burenstam Linder: "Among all nonprimary products, a country has a range of potential exports. This range of exportable products is determined by internal demand. It is a necessary, but not a sufficient, condition that a product be consumed (or invested) in the home country for this product to be a potential export product. This is our basic proposition." An Essay on Trade and Transformation (Stockholm: Almqvist & Wiksell, 1961), p. 87.
2
OECD, Gaps in Technology: Analytical Report (Paris: 1970), p. 197.

3

A similar observation is made by Yoshi Tsurumi: ". . . the sewing machine industries of Japan produced and exported zig-zag automatic models to the United States about four years before Japanese consumers began to trade their straight-stitching models in for zig-zag automatic models. The manufacturers of television sets of Japan produced and exported color television sets to North America almost five years before Japanese consumers began to replace their monochrome television sets with color sets." "Japanese Multinational Firms," Journal of World Trade Law, Vol. 7, No. 1 (January-February 1973), p. 78.

4

This point is stressed in Terutomo Ozawa, "The Import-Pulling Effect of U.S. Marketing and Induced Exports from Low-Wage Countries," a paper presented at the 1968 annual meeting of the Southwestern and Rocky Mountain Division of the American Association for the Advancement of Science.

5

Raymond Vernon, "Solutions: Trade Policy," in Seymour E. Harris, ed., The Dollar in Crisis (New York: Harcourt, Brace & World, 1961), p. 202.

6

This phenomenon is not restricted to merchandise alone. Any Japanese individual who becomes famous in the United States—whether in science, music, arts, or entertainment—is sure to be an instant celebrity in Japan.

7

"Foreign Capital Induction," The Oriental Economist, February 1959, p. 70. A close direct relation between Japan's export growth and technology imports for the period 1950–1963 was statistically detected and examined in Terutomo Ozawa, "Imitation, Innovation; and Japanese Exports," Peter B. Kenen and Roger Lawrence, eds., The Open Economy: Essays on International Trade and Finance (New York: Columbia University Press, 1968), pp. 190–212.

8

A detailed analysis of the keiretsu groups is presented in K. Bieda, The Structure and Operation of the Japanese Economy (Sydney: John Wiley and Sons, 1970), pp. 208–221.

9

Japan Economic Planning Agency, Economic Survey of Japan (1961–1962) (Tokyo: The Japan Times, LTD., 1963), p. 27.

10

In 1970, for example, the export/GNP ratio for Japan was 11.2 percent in contrast to 5.3 percent for the United States, 17.8 percent for France, 22.0 percent for West Germany, and 22.3 percent for the United Kingdom. The ratios are computed from IMF, International Financial Statistics (Washington: IMF, 1970).

11

Leon Hollerman, "Recent Difficulties in Japan's Economic Development,"
Banca Nazionale del Lavoro Quarterly Review, N. 88 (March 1969), p. 8.

12

Ibid. Also see Leon Hollerman, Japan's Dependence on the World Economy: The Approach Toward Economic Liberalization (Princeton: N.J.:
Princeton University Press, 1967).

13

See, for example, Hisao Kanamori, "Economic Growth and Exports," in
L. Klein and K. Ohkawa, eds., Economic Growth (Homewood, Ill.: Irwin,
1968); G. C. Allen, Japan as a Market and Source of Supply (Oxford: Per-
gamon, 1967); and W. W. Lockwood, The Economic Development of Japan (Princeton: Princeton University Press, 1954). Tuvia Blumenthal, on
the other hand, presents some convincing evidence that the role played by
exports in promoting Japan's economic growth during the postwar period
has been grossly underestimated: "Exports and Economic Growth: The
Case of Postwar Japan," Quarterly Journal of Economics, Vol. 86, No. 4
(November 1972), pp. 617–631.

14

In this connection, the following observation made by OECD is relevant:
". . . in the last 40 years, industrial R & D activities have tended to concentrate on the same industrial sectors; chemicals, electrical and nonelectrical machinery, and transportation, all of which have relatively high rates of
commercialization of new products. Innovative activity in industry con-
tributes to productivity increases not only through the development of
new and better production processes, but also through developing new and
better producers' goods, which play an important role in increasing productivity in the industries that purchase them." (OECD, Gaps in Technology,
p. 184).

15

The strong motivation of the Japanese to improve the quality of exports is
discussed in Chapter 7.

16

Japanese Ministry of International Trade and Industry, 1972-Tsuhshoh
Hakusho Kakuron [1972-White Paper on International Trade and Indus-
try] (Tokyo: MITI, 1972), p. 3. Chemicals are treated as manufactured
goods.

Chapter 4

1

OECD, Liberalization of International Capital Movements: Japan (Paris:
1968), pp. 57–58.

2

Stephen Hymer, "International Operations of National Firms—A Study of

Direct Foreign Investment," unpublished Ph.D. dissertation, Massachusetts Institute of Technology, 1960.

3

Ibid., p. 51.

4

The phenomenon of "excessive competition" is discussed by James C. Abegglen and William V. Rapp in "Japanese Managerial Behavior and 'Excessive Competition'," The Developing Economies, Vol. 8, No. 4 (December 1970), pp. 427–444.

5

In 1960, for example, the payment of fees and royalties accounted for about 18 percent of total invisible trade payments, although some payments which are not directly related to technology imports are included in the statistics: The Bank of Japan, Economic Statistics of Japan, 1964.

6

James C. Abegglen, "Changing Japan: Its Challenge to U.S. Industry," The McKinsey Quarterly, fall 1964, p. 5.

7

From October 1956 until June 1963, no official approval was required for these investments made by nonresidents on the condition that neither income nor liquidation proceeds would be transferable abroad. These investments were, however, restricted to the so-called "nonrestricted" industries (that is, industries other than banks, electricity, gas and water utilities, railways and other transport utilities, maritime transport, mining, radio and television, fishing, road construction, port and harbor operations and trustee businesses.)

8

National Industrial Conference Board, Foreign Licensing Agreements, (New York: 1958), pp. 56–58.

9

The Japanese Ministry of International Trade and Industry, Gaishikei Kigyo [Foreign Affiliated Enterprises], 1968, p. 274.

10

K. Bieda, The Structure and Operation of the Japanese Economy (Sydney: John Wiley and Sons, 1970), p. 224.

11

Ibid.

12

"The mechanism by which Japan's enormous postwar expansion has been financed in the face of a capital shortage is in itself conducive to mergers, especially during times of recession or even during a pause in the rate of expansion. At such critical times, the prerogatives and policies of the banks become paramount. Typically, to shore up their own investments, they then salvage those of their clients on the brink of bankruptcy by forcing

mergers between them and more solvent clients—the latter being in no position to resist since they too operate with a high proportion of borrowed funds. In boom times, leading banks follow the complementary policy of sponsoring affiliation among their clients in order to create viable industrial empires; each of these, with a bank symbiotically at its head, may then hope to survive the aggressive expansionary drive of rival empires." Leon Hollerman, Japan's Dependence on the World Economy: The Approach Toward Economic Liberalization, pp. 252–253, copyright 1967 by Princeton University Press, reprinted by permission of the publisher.
13
The Japanese Science and Technology Agency, 1971-White Paper on Science and Technology, p. 79.
14
For a concise analysis of the Japanese government's policy on direct capital imports during the 1960s, see M. Y. Yoshino, "Japan as Host to the International Corporation," in Charles P. Kindleberger, ed., The International Corporation: A Symposium, (Cambridge: The MIT Press, 1970), pp. 345–369.
15
These paragraphs are quoted from Herbert Glazer, The International Businessman in Japan (Rutland, Vermont & Tokyo: C. E. Tuttle Co., 1968), p. 18 and p. 38 respectively, copyright Sophia University, Tokyo.
16
Business Asia, June 2, 1972, p. 176. It also reports: "During the first half of fiscal 1971 (ending March 31, 1971), the FTC examined 708 technical license agreements and found 57 cases in which unfair restrictions were allegedly imposed on licensees."
17
The profitability of foreign-affiliated enterprises mentioned here was reported in "Industrial Roundup," The Oriental Economist, August, 1971, p. 53.
18
". . . there are more than 1.3 million retail shops and 281,000 wholesalers, with some 7.3 million workers. The overwhelming majority of these establishments are small enterprises of fewer than five employees." M. Y. Yoshino, The Japanese Marketing System: Adaptation and Innovations (Cambridge: The MIT Press, 1971), p. 254.
19
The Japan Economic Journal, March 6, 1973.

Chapter 5
1
Koichi Emi, "Economic Development and Educational Investment in the

Meiji Era," in M. J. Bowman et al., eds., Readings in the Economics of
Education (Paris: UNESCO, 1968), p. 103.
2
Ibid., p. 95.
3
Ibid., p. 101.
4
Japanese Science and Technology Agency, 1969 White Paper on Science
and Technology, p. 189.
5
OECD, Gaps in Technology: Analytical Report, (Paris: 1970), 119.
6
The other nine industrial countries are the United States, Belgium, France,
Germany, Italy, the Netherlands, the United Kingdom, Sweden, and Canada: OECD, Gaps in Technology, p. 18.
7
For an analysis of industrial R & D in the United States, see Richard R.
Nelson, Merton J. Peck, and Edward D. Kalacheck, Technology, Economic Growth, and Public Policy (Washington, D.C.: The Brookings Institution, 1967).
8
Eli Ginzberg, "Confrontation and Directions," in Eli Ginzberg, ed., Technology and Social Change (New York: Columbia University Press, 1964),
p. 152.
9
The development of Japan's semiconductor industry is examined in John E.
Tilton, International Diffusion of Technology: The Case of Semiconduc-
tors (Washington, D.C.: The Brookings Institution, 1971). He describes the
research characteristics of Japanese firms in this industry as follows: "In
allocating R & D resources, Japanese firms with few exceptions have
stressed development and engineering projects. Modern central research
laboratories at Hitachi, Nippon Electric, Matsushita, Toshiba, and Mitsubishi Electric, with some of Japan's best technical talent, have concentrated largely on minor advances in proven technology, often with relatively short payoff periods. This emphasis has produced many ingenious
additions to imported technology but few major advances.

This R & D strategy . . . has used Japan's limited R & D resources efficiently. But in recent years, the cost, restrictions, and difficulties encountered in obtaining foreign technology have increased. In addition, as Japanese technology has advanced rapidly, approaching the best technology
found abroad in many fields, the pool of foreign know-how the country
can draw on for further advances in its technology has dwindled. As a result, the government is now stressing the need for more research, and the

traditional R & D strategy may be changing." (pp. 139–140. Copyright 1971 by The Brookings Institution, reprinted by permission of the publisher.)

10

Donald G. Fink, "Human Factors in Transference of Government R & D for Commercial Application," U.S. Congress, Senate, Select Committee on Small Business, The Role and Effect of Technology in the Nation's Economy: Hearings, 88th Congress, Washington, 1964, p. 398.

11

A remark made by Richard S. Morse at a panel discussion on transference of government sponsored R & D to commercial applications. U.S. Congress, Senate, Select Committee on Small Business, The Role and Effect of Technology in the Nation's Economy, p. 384.

12

Daniel L. Spencer, "An External Military Presence, Technological Transfer, and Structural Change," Kyklos, Vol. XVIII, 1965-Fasc. 3, pp. 451–474. Another study on transfers of military technology to Japan was made by G. R. Hall and R. E. Johnson; "Transfers of United States Aerospace Technology to Japan," in Raymond Vernon, ed., The Technology Factor in International Trade (New York: National Bureau of Economic Research, 1970), pp. 305–358.

13

Ibid., p. 465.

14

The Japan Economic Journal, October 10, 1972.

15

Japanese Ministry of Small and Medium-Size Enterprises, 1972 White Paper on Small and Medium-Size Enterprises, (Tokyo: Printing Office, The Ministry of Finance, 1972) p. 269.

16

"Old Japanese Custom," The Economist, January 13, 1962, p. 151.

17

The Japan Economic Journal, July 4, 1972.

18

"Year of the Open Door: The Economist Reconsiders Japan," The Economist, November 28, 1964, p. 1013. Daniel L. Spencer attributes the success of Japan's shipbuilding industry to the adaptations of U.S.-oriented technologies, especially automatic welding: "Automatic welding was developed in the United States under pressure of World War II needs, and the apparatus was manufactured by the Linde Products Division of Union Carbide Corporation. With the permission and encouragement of the American military authorities governing Japan during the Occupation, this engineer secured clearance to visit the United States and Linde Products

Division, where he purchased several automatic welding machines and received several weeks of free instruction in their use. After returning to Japan, he held seminars to teach his fellow engineers what he had learned, and put the machines into operation. With this engineer's help and that of his new contacts at the Linde firm, the Japanese obtained a license to produce welding machines of their own. The phenomenal growth of the Japanese shipbuilding industry to its dominance of producing more than half of the world's ships annually can be ascribed to many factors, including the use of American assembly-line techniques which the Japanese learned from the aircraft and automobile technology transfers. However, Japan's growth as a shipbuilder is inconceivable without these automatic welding machines." Technology Gap in Perspective, (New York: Spartan Books, 1970), pp. 85-86.

19
William Gruber, Dileep Mehta, and Raymond Vernon, "The R & D Factor in International Trade and International Investment of United States Industries," The Journal of Political Economy, Vol. 75, No. 1 (February 1967), pp. 20-48.

20
Another study on the effect of Japan's R & D on export performance—within the framework of the product life cycle theory of trade—is made by Yoshihiro Tsurumi: "R & D Factors and Exports of Manufactured Goods of Japan," in Louis T. Wells, Jr., ed., The Product Life Cycle and International Trade (Boston: Division of Research, Graduate School of Business Administration, Harvard University, 1972), pp. 159-189. He argues that Japan often takes advantage of the duality of its export market by exporting R & D-based products first to Asian markets for test at the early stage of development but later in the maturity stage to other advanced countries.

21
These estimates are computed by the Japanese government in 1970-White Paper on Technology and Science (Tokyo: Printing Office, The Ministry of Finance, 1971), pp. 276-277.

22
In Chapter 4 we noted that Japan's R & D funds rose at the average annual rate of 20.6 percent over the period of 1961-1970, surpassing all other major countries.

23
Japanese Economic Planning Agency, Survey of Public Preferences-August, 1971, quoted in Japanese Science and Technology Agency, 1972 White Paper on Science and Technology, (Tokyo: Printing Office, The Ministry of Finance, 1973), p. 4.

24
Ibid., pp. 20-23.

25
"Industrial Roundup," The Oriental Economist, August 1972, p. 43.
26
"Technology: world markets widen for Japan's newest and fast-growing
export," Business Abroad, November 1970, p. 26.
27
"Technology: A Cleaner Way to Make Coke," Business Week, July 31,
1971, p. 42.
28
For example, Japan even exports garbage disposal technology: "Tezuka
Kosan Company of Tokyo, an oil-pressure press manufacturer, has announced signing contracts to export its wastes disposal equipment and
manufacturing technology to West Germany's Krupp-Braun-Kohle group
and Italy's Worthington, a pump manufacturer. Tezuka's disposal process,
claimed to be unprecedented in the world, involves compressing garbage
into one-fifth its original size by an oil-pressure cylinder, packaging it by
meshed wire and coating it with hot asphalt. Trash thus treated can be
used for landfill and other uses . . . it can handle plastics and junk cars,
which are hard to be burned, and is free from secondary pollution. [The
company] has drawn patents on the process in West Germany, Britain,
France and Italy, and has them pending in the United States," The Japan
Economic Journal, Oct. 31, 1972. It is also reported that according to
one estimate, Japan is spending $50 per capital to control pollution,
whereas the United States is spending $16 per capita: The Journal of
Commerce, Nov. 16, 1972.
29
"Makers of industrial robots have been swamped with inquiries from
European firms for conclusion of agreements for technological exchanges
and sales and technological tie-ups for such robots," The Japan Economic
Journal, July 4, 1972. Inquiries from Russia were reported in the same
Journal, Nov. 7, 1972.
30
The Japan Economic Journal, December 4, 1973.
31
The Japan Economic Journal, October 9, 1973.

Chapter 6
1
Japan Times, April 12, 1972.
2
Industrial Development and Investment Center, the Republic of China,
Overseas Investments in the Republic of China (Taipei: 1971).
3
This general distinction is revealed in Japanese Science and Technology

Agency, Gijutsuyushutsu ni kansuru Chosa Hohkoku [Survey Report on Technology Export] , (Tokyo: 1964).
4
This taxonomy was made by G. R. Hall and R. E. Johnson: "General technology refers to information common to an industry, profession, or trade. At one extreme this category includes such basic skills as arithmetic, and at the other such specialized skills as blueprint reading, tool design, and computer programming. The same general knowledge is processed by all firms in an industry and hence is the ticket of admission to the industry.

System-specific technology refers to the information possessed by a firm or individuals within a firm that differentiates each firm from its rivals, and gives a firm its competitive edge.

Firm-specific knowledge differs from system-specific knowledge in that it cannot be attributed to any specific item the firm produces. Firm-specific knowledge results from the firm's overall activities. Some organizations possess technical knowledge that goes beyond the general information possessed by the industry as a whole; another firm manufacturing the same products would not necessarily acquire this same technology . . . "Transfers of United States Aerospace Technology to Japan," in Raymond Vernon, ed., The Technology Factor in International Trade (New York: National Bureau of Economic Research, 1970), p. 308.
5
Admittedly, there is a greater chance for human conflict because of the large number of direct investments made by the Japanese and their close interactions with local workers. Besides, other Asians view the Japanese as their brothers and tend to expect more from the Japanese than from the Westerners in technical assistance.
6
The Japan Economic Journal, October 10, 1972.
7
Business Asia, December 18, 1970, p. 57.
8
The Japan Economic Journal, November 21, 1972.
9
Ibid.
10
The Japan Economic Journal, November 14, 1972.
11
Nippon Keizai Shimbun, May 9, 1972.
12
It should be noted that U.S. labor can be managed by American managers. The problem is that overseas Japanese companies are mostly reluctant to use local managers largely because of their close relationship with their home offices.

13
The Japan Economic Journal, March 20, 1973.
14
An analysis of Japan's labor-resource-oriented investments in other Asian countries prior to the monetary crises of 1972 is presented in Terutomo Ozawa, "Labor-Resource-Oriented Migration of Japanese Industries to Taiwan, Singapore and South Korea," Economics Staff Working Paper No. 134, International Bank for Reconstruction and Development, August 1972.
15
For factors behind Japan's export efforts from neighboring Asian countries to the United States and Europe, see Terutomo Ozawa, "Multinationalism, Japanese Style," Columbia Journal of World Business, Vol. 7, No. 6 (November–December 1972), pp. 33–42.
16
The Wall Street Journal, June 20, 1973.
17
"International Outlook," Business Week, August 11, 1973, p. 56.
18
The Japan Economic Journal, July 17, 1973.
19
The company's operation is reported in "Japan's foreign investment machine," Business Week, March 24, 1973, p. 57.
20
The story is based on Mr. Tamura's interview with NMB officials. It is reported in his excellent Master's thesis, "Japanese Direct Investment in the United States: Opportunities for Future Growth," submitted to Alfred P. Sloan School of Management, the Massachusetts Institute of Technology, 1973.
21
These experiences of NMB are described in Ibid., pp. 109–112.
22
"Japan' Textile makers widen their U.S. beachhead," Business Week, November 24, 1973, pp. 36–37.

Chapter 7
1
G. B. Sansom, The Western World and Japan (New York: Alfred A. Knopf, © 1950), p. 385.
2
For an authoritative analysis of the social characteristics of the Japanese, see Chie Nakane, Japanese Society (Berkeley: University of California Press, 1970).

3

Quoted in "Business Abroad: An Auto Industry Goes into Shock," Business Week, August 7, 1971, p. 34.

4

An excellent analysis of the unbalanced trade relationship between the United States and Japan is made by Warren S. Hunsberger, "Japan-United States Trade—Patterns, Relationships, Problems," in Jerome B. Cohen, ed., Pacific Partnership: United States-Japan Trade (Lexington, Mass.: D.C. Heath & Co., 1972) pp. 117–148.

5

It has even been said that its true reserves were in the neighborhood of $25 billion, since under the IMF accounting system official deposits with commercial banks and official holdings of foreign bonds are not counted as part of a country's official reserves.

6

Quoted in Donald Kirk, "The Birds around Mount Fuji are Decreasing in Numbers," The New York Times Magazine, March 26, 1972, p. 78.

7

For example, a 1972 survey conducted by the Japan Economic Council indicates that 70 percent of the respondents cited the stabilization of consumer prices as their top concern and that 60 percent expressed their preference for conservation of nature rather than economic growth: The Japan Economic Journal, March 13, 1973.

8

OECD, The Industrial Policy of Japan (Paris: 1972), p. 19.

9

Ibid., p. 16.

10

Louis Kraar, "Japan Sets Out to Remodel Itself," Fortune, March 1973, pp. 98–101.

11

OECD, The Industrial Policy of Japan, pp. 20–21.

12

Eli Ginzberg, "Confrontation and Directions," in Eli Ginzberg, ed., Technology and Social Change (New York: Columbia University Press, 1964), p. 152.

Chapter 8

1

Figures are from Survey of Current Business, March, 1973, Vol. 53, No. 3, p. 23.

2

Michael Boretsky, "Concerns About the Present American Position in

International Trade," <u>Technology and International Trade</u> (Washington,
D.C.: National Academy of Engineering, 1971), pp. 18-66.
3
"Technology and the Trade Crisis: Salvation Through a New Policy?",
<u>Science</u>, Vol. 179, March 2, 1973, p. 882.
4
How each of the six main projects proposed by Nixon failed to be implemented is discussed in "Commentary/Technology—Why the White House
shelved 'a strong new effort'," <u>Business Week</u>, March 3, 1973, p. 36. But a
part of President Nixon's ETIP appears now to be carried out; the government is going to set new tough standards for the $2 billion annual pur-
chases by the General Services Administration so as to encourage product
improvement. The first series of production specifications will reportedly
cover air conditioners (more cool air for the same power consumption)
and power mowers (less noise). "A federal spur to product development,"
<u>Business Week</u>, August 25, 1973, pp. 68-69.
5
The causes of the changing attitude of the public toward science and technology are discussed by Edwin Mansfield in <u>Technological Change</u> (New
York: W. W. Norton & Co., 1971), pp. 151-152.
6
"R & D is losing its high priority," <u>Business Week</u>, May 12, 1973, p. 198.
7
For analysis of the role of advertising and promotional measures in modern
U.S. economy, see, for example, John K. Galbraith, <u>The New Industrial
State</u> (New York: The New American Library, 1968), pp. 208-220.
8
"Since we live in an age of such unquestioning and often very justified
faith in the virtues of innovation, there can develop in the more com-
mitted companies a strongly one-sided system of rewards. Plaudits, Brownie
points, and promotions go to the clearly innovative individuals—and rightly
so. But it is well to be aware of the possible negative consequences. The
most unhappily negative effect may be the creation of an environment in
which people who frequently suggest imitative practices get viewed as
being somehow inferior or less worthy." Theodore Levitt, "Innovative
Imitation," <u>Harvard Business Review</u>, Vol. 44, No. 5 (September–October),
1966, pp. 69-70.
9
This interesting development is documented in "A Return Flow of Technology from Abroad," <u>Fortune</u>, Vol. 88, No. 2, August 1973, p. 63.
10
Harvey Brooks, "What's happening to the U.S. lead in technology?"
<u>Harvard Business Review</u>, Vol. 50, No. 3 (May–June 1972), p. 118.

11

This integrative effect of technology is pointed out by Victor Basiuk, Technology and World Power, Headline Series No. 200, April, 1970, (New York: The Foreign Policy Association), pp. 5–10.

12

This section and the following sections are partly based upon Terutomo Ozawa, "Should the United States Restrict Technology Trade with Japan?" MSU–Business Topics, Vol. 20, No. 4, Autumn, 1972, pp. 35–44.

13

John Stuart Mill, Principles of Political Economy. See, for example, the collected edition of his works by the University of Toronto, Collected Works: John Stuart Mill (Toronto: University of Toronto Press, 1965), Vol. II, pp. 592–593.

14

"Making U.S. Technology More Competitive," Business Week, January 15, 1972, p. 45.

15

Japanese Ministry of International Trade and Industry, Gaishikei Kigyo [Foreign Affiliated Enterprises] , 1968, p. 274.

16

"Economic Woes Aside, Americans Don't Want Japanese Buying Maple," The Wall Street Journal, February 8, 1972.

17

For example, see "Cracking Down: Trustbusters Challenge U.S. Firms' Dealings With Concerns Abroad," The Wall Street Journal, July 30, 1970.

18

In fact, the Justice Department even suggested how business firms might bypass some of the trade obstacles of antitrust regulations. See "Do the antitrust laws really cramp foreign trade?", Business Week, March 10, 1973, p. 75.

19

James C. Abegglen and William V. Rapp, "The Competitive Impact of Japanese Growth," in Jerome B. Cohen, ed., Pacific Partnership: United States–Japan Trade (Lexington, Mass.: Lexington Books, 1972), p. 21.

Index